Five Chimneys

THE STORY OF AUSCHWITZ

By

OLGA LENGYEL

Martino Fine Books
Eastford, CT
2019

Martino Fine Books
P.O. Box 913,
Eastford, CT 06242 USA

ISBN   978-1-68422-393-0

Copyright 2019
Martino Fine Books

Cover Design Tiziana Matarazzo

Printed in the United States of America On 100% Acid-Free Paper

Five Chimneys

THE STORY OF AUSCHWITZ

By
OLGA LENGYEL

CHICAGO NEW YORK

ZIFF-DAVIS PUBLISHING COMPANY

Acknowledgments

The Author is indebted to Louis Zara for his splendid co-operation and constructive suggestions and to Isidore Lipschutz and Oscar Ray for their invaluable assistance. Thanks are also due to Clifford Coch for translating from the French edition of the same work, to Paul P. Weiss for translating the balance from Hungarian, and to the Publisher and the Editorial Staff for many constructive suggestions and for making possible the American publication of this book.

Contents

CHAPTER I

8 Horses — or 96 Men, Women, and Children

Mea culpa, my fault, *mea maxima culpa!* I cannot acquit myself of the charge that I am, in part, responsible for the destruction of my own parents and of my two young sons. The world understands that I could not have known, but in my heart the terrible feeling persists that I could have, I might have, saved them.

It was 1944, nearly five years after Hitler had invaded Poland. Everywhere the Gestapo ruled, and Germany fattened on the loot of the continent, for two-thirds of Europe lay under the talons of the Third Reich. We lived in Cluj,[1] a city of 100,000, the capital of Transylvania. Formerly it had belonged to Rumania, but the Vienna Award of 1940 had transferred it to Hungary, also one of the New Order's satellite countries. The Germans were the masters, and though one hardly dared to hope, we sensed — nay, we prayed — that the day of reckoning was not far off. Meanwhile, we tried to stifle our fears and go about our daily tasks, avoiding, whenever possible, any contact with them. We knew that we were at the mercy of ruthless men — and women, too, as we later learned — but no one could have convinced us then how truly pitiless they could be.

My husband, Miklos Lengyel, was the director of his own hospital, "Doctor Lengyel's Sanatorium," a modern two-story seventy-bed institution, which we had built in 1937. He had

---

[1] The Germans called it Klausenburg; the Hungarians, who had held it prior to 1918, knew it as Kolozsvar.

1

studied in Berlin, where he had given much time to the charity clinics. Now he specialized in general surgery and gynecology. Extremely skillful, and devoted to his science, he was widely respected. He was not a political man, although he understood fully that we were in the center of a maelstrom and in constant peril. He had no leisure for outside occupations. Frequently he had to see 120 patients in a single day and was in surgery till the far hours of the night. But Cluj was a thriving community, and we were proud to operate one of its chief hospitals.

I, too, was devoted to medicine. I had attended the University in Cluj and had qualified to be my husband's first surgical assistant. Indeed, I had helped to furnish the new hospital, bringing to its *decor* a woman's love for color; and so had brightened the appointments in the most advanced manner. Yet, although I had a career, I was even prouder of my little family, for we had two sons, Thomas and Arvad. No one, I thought, could be happier than we were. In our home resided my parents and also my godfather, Professor Elfer Aladar, a famous internist who was engaged in cancer research.

The first years of the war had been relatively calm for us, though we listened with dread to the never-ending accounts of the Reichswehr's triumphs. As they ravaged more and more territories, doctors and, especially, capable surgeons to serve the civilian populace became fewer. My husband, though prudent and sufficiently circumspect, made little effort to conceal his hope that the cause of humanity might not be entirely engulfed. Naturally, he spoke freely only to his confidants, but corruptible souls lurked in every circle and one never knew who might next turn informer. However, the authorities in Cluj left him in peace.

As early as the winter of 1939 we caught an inkling of what was going on inside the lands which the Nazis had occupied. At that time we gave sanctuary to a number of Polish refugees who had fled their homes after their armies were surrounded. We listened, we sympathized, and we helped. Nevertheless,

2

we could not fully credit everything that we heard. These people were overwrought and distracted; they might be exaggerating.

As late as 1943 frightening accounts reached us of atrocities committed inside the concentration camps in Germany. But, like so many of those who listen to me today, we could not believe stories so horrible. We still looked upon Germany as a nation which had given much culture to the world. If these tales were at all true, the shameful acts must be due to a handful of madmen; this could not be national policy, nor part of a plan for global mastery. How little we understood!

Even when a German Major in the Wehrmacht, who was billeted in our home, spoke of the fog of terror with which his country had blanketed Europe, we could not accept it. He was not an uneducated man; I was therefore convinced that he was trying to frighten us. We tried to live apart from him, until one evening he demanded to be admitted to our company. It seemed that he sought only conversation, but the longer he spoke the more bitterness he spewed out. Everywhere, he declared, the subject peoples gazed at him with eyes that brimmed with hatred. Yet from his family at home he received only complaints that he was not sending back enough loot! Other soldiers, privates and officers, were sending home so much more in jewelry, clothes, objects of art, and food.

I had to listen. What impressed me was his violent self-hatred as he told of marching his troops down roads that were literally flanked by bodies swinging from gallows. I vowed that he was either mad or drunk, though I knew that he was neither. He told of motor vans, constructed expressly to gas prisoners. He spoke of huge camps devoted solely to the extermination of civilian minorities by the millions. My flesh crawled. How could anyone believe such fantastic tales?

We did have a few alarming experiences in Cluj, and, as I reflect now, I am sure that any one of these should have been a warning. The most serious occurred in early 1944. One

3

day my husband was called to the police station for interrogation by the feared S.S. He was accused specifically of boycotting the use of German pharmaceutical preparations in his clinic.

Representatives of the German Bayer Company, many of whom were secretly members of the S.S., moved freely through Transylvania, to their personal profit, and to further the expansion of their firm. They had built a network of espionage, and a man who owned a large hospital, and was probably no friend of the Third Reich, was an easy target.

Fortunately, Dr. Lengyel was able to supply a plausible explanation, and the S.S. released him. Privately, we agreed that the questioning must have been prompted by a denunciation. We were even certain that we knew the envious colleague who was responsible.

That episode should have prepared us for what followed. However, we could not imagine how cunningly the German masters laid their plans. They baited many traps, but they wanted a big haul for their trouble.

The first week in May, Dr. Lengyel was again summoned to the police station. I became apprehensive the moment he left the clinic. When he did not return soon I made inquiries. Almost as though in a dream I received the news that he was to be deported to Germany *immediately*.

Frantically, I sought more information. All that I could learn was that he was to be sent away by train inside of an hour.

What went through my mind? My husband was a distinguished surgeon. Doubtless there was a shortage of medical men in Germany. He would be put to work in some metropolitan hospital or clinic. I asked where, and got only a shrug for a reply. I asked if the authorities would permit me to accompany him. The S.S. official blandly declared that they had no objection. If I chose to go, I was welcome. Indeed, they intimated that there was nothing to fear. So in a dozen little ways they mollified, and even encouraged me.

Instantly my decision was made. We would have to face

4

many hardships; the pleasant life we had known might well be ended for years. But separation would be even worse. The war might continue for months, for years. The front lines were always shifting, and we might be cut away from each other forever. By going together we would at least be assured a common fate. In the future, as in the past, my place would be at the side of my husband.

How fatal was to be this move which I was making so deliberately! For before half an hour had passed I was to become the author of my parents' misfortunes, and of my children's as well.

For my parents tried to convince me to stay. "After all," reasoned my father, who had formerly been director of coal mines in Transylvania, "if your husband were called to the colors as a soldier, you would not be able to follow him."

I insisted. After all, had I not received assurances from a German officer that there was no danger?

There was no time for debate. The hour was nearly over. Seeing that I could not be dissuaded, my parents, too, decided to accompany us. Of course, we could not leave the two children behind. Hastily, we threw a few valuables and the usual articles for a journey into a valise, hailed a taxi, and dashed off to join my husband. He was being held at the municipal prison.

We had no inkling of the treachery of which we were the victims until we all stood together on the platform in the railroad depot. Then we discovered that hosts of neighbors and friends were there, too. Many other men had been similarly arrested and their families encouraged to go with them. Still it was not too alarming. The Germans were thorough. They had used the same technique. Why? We were puzzled, baffled, heavy-hearted, but there was no one to ask. Suddenly we learned that the entire station was encircled by hundreds of soldiers. Someone voiced a desire to turn back, but the phalanx of grim sentries made that impossible. We clutched each others' hands and tried to be cool for the children's sake.

There was a nightmarish quality to the scene. On the tracks, an endless train waited. Not passenger coaches but cattle cars, each filled to bursting with candidates for deportation. We stared. People called to each other fearfully. The insignia on the cars indicated their points of origin: Hungary, Yugoslavia, Rumania — only God knew where this train had first been assembled.

Protest was useless. It was our turn. The soldiers began to close in and push us. Like sheep we were driven and compelled to climb into an empty cattle car. We tried only to keep together as we were wedged in. Then the single door was rolled shut behind us. I do not remember whether we wept or shouted. The train was under way.

Ninety-six persons had been thrust into our car, including many children who were squeezed in among the luggage — the pitifully meager luggage that contained only what was most precious or useful. Ninety-six men, women, and children in a space that would have accommodated only eight horses. Yet that was not the worst.

We were so crowded that half our number had no place to sit. Pressed against one another, my husband, my older son, and I remained standing to provide a space for my father. He had undergone a serious operation a short time before and absolutely had to rest.

Besides, as the first hour and then the second passed, we perceived that the simplest details of existence would be extremely complicated. Sanitary disposal was out of the question. Fortunately, several mothers had had the foresight to bring chamber pots for their young. With a blanket for a curtain, we isolated one corner of the car. We could empty the bowls through the single tiny window, but we had no water with which to rinse them. We called for help, but there was no answer. The train moved on — toward the unknown.

As the journey stretched endlessly, the car jerking and jolting, all the forces of nature conspired against us ninety-six. A

6

torrid sun heated the walls until the air became suffocating. The interior was almost completely black, for the daylight that filtered through the little window sufficed to light only that corner. After a while we decided that it was better that way. The scene was becoming more and more unattractive.

The travelers were mostly persons of culture and position from our community. Many were Jewish doctors, or other professional men, and members of their families. In the beginning, everyone tried, despite the common terror, to be courteous and helpful. But as the hours slipped away the veneers cracked. Soon there were incidents and, later, serious quarrels. Thus, little by little, the atmosphere was poisoned. The children cried; the sick groaned; the older people lamented; and even those who, like me, were in perfect health, began to pay attention to their own discomforts. The trip was incredibly morbid and gloomy, and although the same could have been said of every other car on our train, and indeed, of the innumerable trains from every corner of Europe — from France, Italy, Belgium, Holland, Poland, the Ukraine, the Baltic countries, and the Balkans — which were all moving toward the same inhuman destination, we knew only our own problems.

Soon the situation was intolerable. Men, women, and children were struggling hysterically for every square inch. As night fell we lost all concept of human behavior and the wrangling increased until the car was a bedlam.

Finally, the cooler heads prevailed and a semblance of order was restored. A doctor and I were chosen captains-in-charge. Our task was herculean: to maintain the most elementary discipline and hygiene, to care for the sick, to calm those who were agitated, and to control those who went berserk. Above all, it was our duty to maintain the morale of the company, an utterly impossible assignment, for we ourselves were on the border of despair.

A thousand practical problems had to be solved. The food problem was overwhelming. Our guards gave us nothing, and the slender provisions we had brought along began to give out. It was the third day. My heart rose in my throat. Already three days! How much longer? And where were we bound? Worst of all was the knowledge that many of our companions had concealed part of their food. They naively believed that they would be put to work upon arrival at our destination, and that they would need what they had to supplement the regular rations. Fortunately, our misery reduced our appetites. But we observed a rapid deterioration in the general health of the group. Those who had been weak or ailing when we started were suffering, and even the hale were weakening.

The head of an S.S. guard appeared at the window. His Luger gestured threateningly. "Thirty wrist watches, right away. If not, you may all consider yourselves dead!"

He had come for his first collection of a German "tax," and we had to supply enough valuables to satisfy him. So it was that my little Thomas had to part with the wrist watch we had given him after his successful third-grade examination in school.

"Your fountain pens and your brief cases!"

Another "tax."

"Your jewels, and we will bring you a bucket of fresh water!"

One bucket of water for ninety-six human beings, of which number thirty were small children. That would mean a few drops for each soul, but it would be the first we had tasted in twenty-four hours.

"Water, water!" the sick groaned as the bucket was lowered.

I looked at Thomas, my younger son. He was staring at the water. How parched his lips were! He turned and gazed into my eyes. He, too, understood our predicament. He swallowed his spittle and did not ask for any. He was given nothing to drink, for so many needed the precious drops more then he did. I suffered for him, but I was also proud of his stamina.

Now we had more sick in our car. Two people were tormented by ulcers of the stomach. Two others were stricken with erysipelas. Many were tortured by dysentery.

8

Three children were lying near the door. They looked hot and feverish. One of the doctors examined them and stood back aghast. They were ill with scarlet fever!

A shudder ran through me. In these close quarters the entire company would be exposed to the disease.

It was impossible to isolate the youngsters. The only "quarantine" we could enforce was to have those who were near the infected ones turn their backs.

At first everybody tried to keep away from the sick to avoid contagion. But as the days passed we became indifferent to such dangers.

On the second day one of the leading merchants from Cluj suffered a heart attack. His son, also a doctor, knelt beside him. Without drugs he was powerless, and could only watch his father expire while the train rattled on.

Death in the car! A gasp of horror ran through the tightly packed mass of humans.

Piously, the son began to murmur the traditional mourners' chant, and many lifted their voices with him.

At the next station the train stopped. The door opened and a Wehrmacht soldier entered. The dead man's son cried, "We have a corpse in our midst. My father has died."

"Keep your corpse," the other returned brutally. "You will have many more of them soon!"

We were shocked at his indifference. But before long we had many more corpses, and after awhile we, too, became so numb and shaken that it did not matter.

"At last," sighed a husband as he lowered the eyelids of his adored wife who had just succumbed.

"My God, how long it takes!" wept a mother as she bent over her dying eighteen-year-old daughter. Was that the fifth, or the sixth, day of the endless journey?

The cattle car had become an abbatoir. More and more prayers for the dead rose in the stifling atmosphere. But the S.S. would neither let us bury nor remove them. We had to live with our corpses around us. The dead, the contagiously ill, those suffering from organic diseases, the parched, the famished, and the mad must all travel together in this wooden gehenna.

On the seventh day my friend Olly attempted suicide by poison. Her children, two adorable little youngsters; her old parents who had originally come to Cluj as refugees from Vienna; and her husband, though a doctor himself, begged Doctor Lengyel to save her.

First of all, he must flush the woman's stomach. For that a rubber tube was indispensable. Luckily, if one can say that, my father had since his operation carried an apparatus for urination which contained a rubber tube. To fetch this tube to poor Olly it was literally necessary to walk on our ailing neighbors. After that, my husband had to administer the treatment in a tiny space without proper instruments and without a light. But the greatest problem was that of water.

At the bottom of a few canteens and gourds, there was still a meager reserve of the precious liquid. No one offered to part with any. It took all the authority my husband commanded to make them give a little up.

In spite of all the handicaps, the treatment was a success and the woman was saved. Temporarily, at least. Alas, the next day she was to be led directly to her death.

From time to time in the course of this infernal trip, I tried to forget reality, the dead, the dying, the stench, and the horrors. I stood on several suitcases and peered out of the little window. I gazed at the enchanting countryside of the Tatras, the magnificent forests of fir trees, the green meadows, the peaceful pastures, and the charming little houses. It was all like a scene advertising Swiss chocolates. How unreal it seemed!

Twice each day, the guards made their check. We thought that they would keep an extremely close watch, for we imagined that they had comprehensive files and were ready to verify the minutest details with the proverbial German thoroughness. This was simply another illusion we were destined to lose. They were interested in us only as a group, and cared nothing whatever about individuals.

Occasionally, we went through stations where troop trains and hospital trains were waiting. The soldiers of the Wehrmacht had an inflated morale. Whether drunk with victory or exasperated by defeat, these troops, both well and wounded, had nothing but ironic sneers for plague-ridden people like deportees in cattle cars. The most uncouth and cruel insults came to our ears. Again and again I asked myself if it was really possible that these men in green knew no emotions but malice and hate. In any case, at no time did I see the slightest manifestation of sympathy or compassion.

Then, at the end of the seventh day, the death car halted. We had arrived. But where? Was this a city? And what would they do to us now?

CHAPTER II

The Arrival

Today, when I think about our arrival at the camp, the cars of our train appear to me as so many coffins. It was, indeed, a funeral train. The S.S. and Gestapo agents were our undertakers; the officers who later evaluated our "riches" were our greedy and impatient heirs.

We could feel nothing but a deep sense of relief. Anything would be better than this terrible uncertainty. In a prison on wheels, could there be anything more appalling than the oppressive gloom, reeking with foul odors, alive with heartbreaking groans and lamentations?

We hoped to be released from the car without delay. But this hope was soon blasted. We were to spend an eighth night in the train, the living piled one on top of another to avoid contact with the decaying corpses.

No one slept that night. Our sense of relief gave way to anxiety as though a sixth sense were warning us of impending disaster.

With difficulty, I ploughed through the compact mass of animal humanity to reach the little window. There I saw a weird spectacle. Outside was a veritable forest of barbed wire, which was illumined at intervals by powerful searchlights.

An immense blanket of light covered everything within view. It was a chilling sight, yet reassuring, too. This lavish expenditure of electricity undoubtedly indicated that civilization was nearby and an end to the conditions we had endured.

Still, I was far from apprehending the true meaning of the display. Where were we and what fate awaited us? I conjectured wisely, yet my imagination could not supply a reasonable explanation.

Finally, I went back to my parents, for I felt a great need to talk to them.

"Can you ever forgive me?" I murmured, as I kissed their hands.

"Forgive you?" asked my mother with her characteristic tenderness. "You have done nothing for which you need to be forgiven."

But her eyes dimmed with tears. What did she suspect in this hour?

"You have always been the best of daughters," added my father.

"Perhaps we shall die," my mother went on quietly, "but you are young. You have the strength to fight, and you will live. You can still do so much for yourself, and the others."

This was to be the last time that I embraced them.

At last the pale day broke. In a little while an official we learned was the camp commandant came to accept us into his custody. He was accompanied by an interpreter who, we later were told, spoke nine languages. The latter's duty was to transmit every instruction into the native tongues of the deportees. He warned us that we were to observe the strictest discipline and carry out every order without discussion. We listened. What reason had we to suspect worse treatment than we had already received?

On the platform, we saw a group in convict-striped uniforms. That sight made a painful impression. Would we become broken, emaciated like these wrecks? They had been brought to the station to take over our luggage, or rather, what remained of it after the guards had exacted their "taxes." Here we were completely dispossessed.

The order came, curt and demanding: "Get out!"

The women were lined up on one side, the men on the other, in ranks of five.

The doctors were to stand by in a separate row with their instrument bags. That was rather reassuring. If doctors were needed, it meant that the sick would receive medical attention. Four or five ambulances drove up. We were told that these would transport the ailing. Another good sign.

How could we know that all this was window-dressing to maintain order among the deportees with a minimum of armed force? We could not possibly have guessed that the ambulances would cart the sick directly to the gas chambers, whose existence I had doubted; and thence to the crematories!

Quieted by such cunning subterfuges, we allowed ourselves to be stripped of our belongings and marched docilely to the slaughter houses.

While we were assembled on the station platform, our luggage was taken down by the creatures in convict stripes. Then the bodies of those who had died on the journey were removed. The corpses that had been with us for days were bloated hideously and in various stages of decomposition. The odors were so nauseating that thousands of flies had been attracted. They fed on the dead and attacked the living, tormenting us incessantly.

As soon as we left the cattle cars, my mother, my sons and I were separated from my father and my husband. We now stood in columns that extended for hundreds of yards. The train had discharged from four to five thousand passengers, all as dazed and bewildered as we were.

More commands, and we were paraded before about thirty S.S. men, including the head of the camp and other officers. They began to choose, sending some of us to the right and some to the left. This was the first "selection," in the course of which, as we could not dream could be true, the initial sacrifices for the crematories were picked.

14

Children and old people were told off automatically, "To the left!" At the moment of parting came those shrieks of despair, those frantic cries, "Mama, Mama!" that will ring forever in my ears. But the S.S. guards demonstrated that they were moved by no sentiments. All those who tried to resist, old or young, they beat mercilessly; and quickly they re-formed our column into the two new groups, right and left, but always in ranks of five.

The only explanation came from an S.S. officer who assured us that the aged would remain in charge of the children. I believed him, assuming naturally that the able-bodied adults would have to work, but that the old and very young would be cared for.

Our turn came. My mother, my sons, and I stepped before the "selectors." Then I committed my second terrible error. The selector waved my mother and myself to the adult group. He classed my younger son Thomas with the children and aged, which was to mean immediate extermination. He hesitated before Arvad, my older son.

My heart thumped violently. This officer, a large dark man who wore glasses, seemed to be trying to act fairly. Later I learned that he was Dr. Fritz Klein, the "Chief Selector."[1] "This boy must be more than twelve," he remarked to me.

"No," I protested.

The truth was that Arvad was not quite twelve, and I could have said so. He was big for his age, but I wanted to spare him from labors that might prove too arduous for him.

"Very well," Klein agreed amiably. "To the left!"

I had persuaded my mother that she should follow the children and take care of them. At her age she had a right to the treatment accorded the elderly and there would be someone to look after Arvad and Thomas.

"My mother would like to remain with the children," I said.

---

[1] In 1945, Dr. Fritz Klein was one of the main attractions at the trial of the Belsen hangmen.

15

"Very well," he again acquiesced. "You'll all be in the same camp."

"And in several weeks you'll all be reunited," another officer added, with a smile. "Next!"

How should I have known? I had spared them from hard work, but I had condemned Arvad and my mother to death in the gas chambers.

*   *   *   *

The road was in good repair. It was the beginning of May and a cool wind carried to us a peculiar, sweetish odor, much like that of burning flesh, although we did not identify it as that. This odor greeted us upon our arrival and stayed with us always.

The "Lager" occupied a vast space of about six by eight miles, as I later verified. It was surrounded by cement posts, ten or twelve feet high and about fifteen inches thick. These stood at intervals of four yards with a double network of barbed wire between them. On each post rose an electric lamp, an enormous bright eye that was leveled at the internees and was never extinguished. Inside the immense enclosure were many camps, each designated by a letter.

The camps were separated by three-foot embankments. On top of these embankments stretched three rows of barbed wire, charged with electric current.

As we entered the grounds of the Lager and the different camps, we distinguished several wooden buildings. The barbed wire which surrounded these structures reminded us of cages. Penned up inside these cages were women in nondescript rags, with their heads shorn of their hair, and their feet bare. In all the languages of Europe, they pleaded for a crust of bread or a shawl to cover their nakedness.

We heard wailing cries.

"You will crack too, like so many of us."

16

"You will be cold and hungry like we are!"

"You will be beaten, too!"

Suddenly a large well-dressed woman appeared in the midst of this herd. With a massive club, she struck at everyone who got in her way.

We could not believe our eyes. Who were these women? What crime had they committed? Where were we?

It was like a nightmare. Was this the courtyard of a mad-house? Perhaps this woman was a warden resorting to her last recourse — the strong arm. "Evidently," I told myself, "these women are abnormals, and that is why they are isolated."

I was still unable to conceive that women of sound mind and guilty of no crimes could be so humiliated and so degraded.

Above all, I was far from imagining that before long I, too, would be reduced to the same pitiful condition.

After waiting about two hours in front of a vast, but coarsely constructed, building, we were thoroughly chilled. Then a troop of soldiers pushed us inside. We found ourselves in a sort of hangar, 25 or 30 feet wide, and about 100 feet long. Here the guards shoved us into a group so tightly pressed together that it was actually painful to move. The big doors closed.

About twenty soldiers, most of whom were drunk, remained inside. They glared and shouted sarcastic comments.

An officer began to bark orders: "Undress! Leave all your clothing here. Leave your papers, valuables, medical equipment; and form rows against the wall."

A murmur of indignation arose. Why should we undress?

"Silence! If you do not want to be beaten within an inch of your lives, hold your tongues!" shouted the officer.

The interpreter translated this into all languages.

"From now on, don't forget that you are prisoners."

The two dozen guards in charge of the unclothing operation, started their work.

At that moment, our last doubts vanished. Now we understood that we had been horribly deceived. The luggage we had

17

left at the station was lost to us forever. The Germans had expropriated everything, even to the smallest souvenirs that could remind us of our past lives. To me the loss of the photographs of my loved ones saddened me most. But our hour of shame had begun.

As we began to undress, weird sensations swept over us. Many of us, doctors or doctors' wives, had provided ourselves with capsules of poison in case of the worst. Why? Because we had lived in an atmosphere of dread and wanted to be prepared for any emergency. Even though I had been optimistic when we left, I, too, had supplied myself with such a weapon of self-destruction. There is some comfort in knowing that, as the last resort, one is master of his own life or death! In a sense this represents the ultimate in liberty. In divesting us of every article the Germans knew they were asking us to give such things up, too.

Immediately, a Hungarian woman, Doctor G., took her syringe of morphine and, as it was impossible to give herself an intravenous injection, swallowed its contents. However, the poison was absorbed by the buccal duct and did not bring the desired effect.

I was consumed by one thought: how could I hide my poison? We were ordered to the baths. We had to walk into another room, completely in the nude except for our shoes, and with open hands while they inspected us. Then luck was with me. We were told to remove our shoes. However, those whose shoes were shabby were allowed to wear them; the Germans would not bother with valueless articles. I was wearing boots, which, at the beginning of spring, were of no interest to the guards, especially since they were covered with mud and dirt. Quickly, in a slit in the lining of a boot, I concealed my greatest treasure, the poison.

"Up against the wall," cried the guards. They struck our naked bodies with their truncheons, as we had seen the woman doing a short time before to those wretched inmates.

18

A few of my neighbors tried desperately to keep their papers — some their prayer books, or photographs. But the guards were eagle-eyed. They slashed out with the iron-tipped clubs, or pulled their hair so hard that the unfortunate women shrieked and collapsed upon the ground.

"You won't need identification papers or photos any more!" cried the mockers.

I lined up in my row, completely naked, my shame engulfed in terror. At my feet lay my clothes, and, on top, the pictures of my family. I looked once more at the faces of my loved ones. My parents, my husband, and my children seemed to be smiling at me . . . . I stooped and slipped these dear images into my crumpled jacket on the ground. My family should not see my horrible degradation.

Around me the frightful agitation, the weeping, and the cowering, continued. In bitterness, I found some satisfaction in ripping my blouse and dress. It may have been a stupid gesture, yet it was a comfort to know that at least my clothing would not be at the disposal of these hideous "supermen."

Now we were compelled to undergo a thorough examination in the Nazi manner, oral, rectal, and vaginal — another horrible experience. We had to lie across a table, stark naked while they probed. All that in the presence of drunken soldiers who sat around the table, chuckling obscenely.

When the examination was over, we were shoved into an adjoining chamber. There followed another interminable period of waiting, before a partition which was marked, "Showers." We shivered from the cold, and from the humiliation. Despite the weariness and the sufferings, many of the women still retained the beauty of their faces and bodies.

Again we had to march before a table where leering German soldiers were seated. We were pushed into another room where men and women, armed with scissors and clippers, waited for us. We were to be clipped and depilated. The clipped hair was accumulated in large sacks, evidently to be utilized for some

19

purpose. Human hair was one of the precious raw materials which German industry needed.[1]

A few women were lucky enough to be worked on with fast-moving clippers. They were envied by those whose hair was cut with scissors, for our barbers were hardly professional. Besides, they were in such haste that they left irregular tufts on the skulls, as though they deliberately sought to make us look ridiculous.

Long before my turn, a German officer singled me out. "Don't clip that one's hair," he said to a guard. The soldier moved me aside, then forgot about me.

I tried to analyze my predicament. What did the officer want from me? I was fearful. Why should I have been the only one whose hair was not cut? Perhaps I would get better treatment. But, no, from this foe one could expect no mercy, except at an ugly price. I did not want to be preferred; it was better to stay with my companions. So I disregarded the order, and got into line to be shorn.

Suddenly the officer reappeared. He gazed at my bare skull, grew angry, and slapped my face as hard as he could. Then he reprimanded the guard, and ordered him to give me a few lashes with his whip. That was the first time I was beaten in the camp. Each blow cut my heart as it did my flesh. We were lost souls. God, where art Thou?

I arrived at that state of numbness where I was no longer sensitive to either club or whip. I lived through the rest of that scene almost as a spectator, thinking only of my boots and of the poison in the lining. Nothing but the thought and the hope that the last word could still be mine bolstered my waning strength.

*　　　　*　　　　*　　　　*

Once the "formalities" of the search were ended, we were

---

[1] They used it to fill cushions and mattresses. The families of the Third Reich slept on the hair of its victims.

herded into the shower room. We passed in rotation, under faucets which sprinkled us with a trickle of hot water. The whole affair did not last more than a minute. Then we were smeared with disinfectant on our heads and on the usual parts of the body. We were not yet dry, when we were led into a third room. The windows and doors were wide open. But, after all, we were in their clutches and our lives obviously meant nothing to anyone.

Here we received our prison clothing. I cannot think of any name that would fit the bizarre rags that were handed out for underwear. We asked ourselves what this "underclothing" was supposed to be. It was not white nor any other color, but worn-out pieces of coarse dusting-cloth. And still we could not be choosy. Only a few of the select were awarded underwear. The majority had to wear their dresses next to their skins.

The dresses, too, made one think of a fantastic masquerade. A few blouses were of convict-striped material. The rest were of rags that may have come from brightly colored gowns, but were now in tatters.

No one cared whether these rags fit the internees. Large, buxom women had to wear little dresses that were too short and too tight and did not come to their knees. Slender women were given huge dresses, some with trains. Yet, despite the absurdity of the distribution, most of the internees, even those who had the chance, refused to exchange their "dresses" with their neighbors. However, there was no way to alter them. Buttons, thread, needles, and safety pins were nonexistent.

To complete the style, the Germans had an arrow of red paint, two inches wide and two feet long, on the back of each garment. We were marked like pariahs.

I drew an ordinary assortment. My new outfit consisted of one of those formerly elegant dresses of tulle, quite tattered and transparent, and without a slip. With that, I was handed a pair of men's drawers of striped fabric. The dress was bare in the front down to the navel and in the back down to the hips.

21

In spite of the tragedy of our situation, we could not help but laugh as we saw the others so ridiculously rigged out. After a while, it was a struggle to overcome the disgust we felt for our companions, and for ourselves.

Thus attired, we were driven into rows in front of the shower building. Once more, we had to wait long hours. No one was permitted to stir. The weather was cold. The skies were lowering. A wind had risen. The dresses, which we had put on while we were still wet, became damp. This first test in endurance was to claim many victims. Cases of pneumonia, otitis, and meningitis were soon to appear, many to prove fatal.

From the old inmates we learned that we were about forty miles west of Krakow. The place was called Birkenau, after the nearby forest of Birkenwald. Birkenau was five miles from the village and camp of Auschwitz, or Oswiecim. The post office was eight miles away in Neuberun.

At last we were marched away. We tramped past a charming forest on the outskirts of which stood a red brick building. Great flames belched from the chimney, and the strange, sickening, sweetish odor which had greeted us upon our arrival, attacked us even more powerfully now.

Logs were piled against the walls for nearly a hundred yards. We asked one of the guides, an old inmate, about this structure.

"It is a camp 'bakery,' " she replied.

We absorbed that without the slightest suspicion. Had she revealed the truth we simply would not have believed her. The bakery which gave off the sickeningly sweetish odor was the crematory, to which the young and the old and the sick had been consigned, and to which ultimately we were all doomed.

CHAPTER III

Barrack 26

We arrived in front of the enclosure to which we had been assigned. The glaring lamps on the barbed wire which encircled the camp indicated that the wires were charged with high-tension current.

The great padlock, which secured the gates, was opened. We shuffled inside. When the last deportees had crossed the threshold the squeaking barrier was closed.

All our past lives remained on the other side of that portal. Hereafter, we would be no more than slaves, always hungry and cold, at the mercy of the guards, and without hope. Tears were in every eye as we followed our guide to our new home, "Barrack 26."

Because both Birkenau and Auschwitz are infamous names and a blot on the history of mankind it is necessary to explain how they differed. The railroad separated one from the other. When the selectors told off the deportees on the station platform "Right!" or "Left!" they were sending them to either Birkenau or Auschwitz. Auschwitz was a slave camp. Hard as life was at Auschwitz it was better than Birkenau. For the latter was definitely an extermination camp, and as such was never mentioned in the reports. It was part of the colossal guilt of the German rulers and was rarely referred to, nor was its existence ever admitted until the troops of the liberating allies exposed the secret to the world.

At Auschwitz many war factories were in operation, such as the D.A.W. (Deutsches-Aufrustungswerk), Siemens, and Krupp. All were devoted to the production of armaments. The prisoners detailed to work there were highly privileged compared to those who were not given such employment. But even those who did not work productively were more fortunate than the prisoners in Birkenau. The latter were merely awaiting their turn to be gassed and cremated. The unpleasant job of handling the soon-to-be corpses, and later the ashes, were relegated to groups called "kommandos." The sole task of the Birkenau personnel was to camouflage the real reason for the camp: *extermination.* When the internees in Auschwitz, or in other camps in the area, were no longer judged useful they were dispatched to Birkenau to die in the ovens. It was as simple and cold-blooded as that.

These details I discovered little by little as the weeks went by. During the first days in the camp we still believed that we would be put to work. For did we not see signs proclaiming *Arbeit macht frei* (Work is freedom)? It was more of the German bear-baiting of their helpless victims. Always they toyed with us, as a cat does with a mouse it surely will kill.

"Barrack 26" was a vast hangar of rough boards which had been thrown together as a stable. On the door a metal plaque gave the number of horses the building would shelter. "Mangy animals are to be separated immediately," it read. How fortunate the horses had been! Nobody ever bothered to take any precautions on behalf of the human beings who were kept there.

The interior was divided into two parts by a large brick stove which was about four feet high. On either side of the stove stood three tiers of bunks.

To be more exact, here stood wooden cages which we called "koias." In each cage, which measured twelve by five feet, seventeen to twenty persons huddled together. There was little comfort to be had in these "bunks."

When we first arrived the koias had nothing but bare boards.

24

Upon these we slept when we could. A month later our masters issued blankets. For each koia two miserably filthy, odorous blankets; that is, one blanket for every ten persons.

Not all of the occupants were able to sleep at the same time, for there was an acute shortage of space. Some had to spend the entire night squatting in awkward positions. Inside a koia the slightest movement was an extremely complicated matter which required the participation, or at least the accord, of all the others who dwelt there.

To make matters worse, the roof of the barrack was in deplorable repair. When it rained, the water leaked in and the internees on the top tiers were literally inundated. But those on the ground level were hardly better off. The ground was cemented only about the stove. There was no floor except the beaten earth, dirty and wet, which the lightest rainfall turned into a sea of mud. Besides, at the lowest level the air was absolutely suffocating.

The filth in the barrack surpassed imagination. Our principal duty was to see to its cleanliness. Any infringement of the hygienic rules was subject to severe sanctions. Yet how ridiculous to expect cleanliness in barrack huts which sheltered from 1,400 to 1,500 women, when we had no broom, no mop, no pail, not even a dust rag. We met the last problem. We decided that one woman, whose dress was particularly long, should have it cut off at the bottom. With this rag we made a feeble mop. It was about time, for the filth on the ground was contaminating the wretched air we breathed.

It was more difficult to solve the problem of dishes. The second day we received about twenty bowls — twenty bowls for 1,500 persons! Each bowl held about one and a half quarts. They also gave us a pail, and a boiler with a capacity of five quarts.

The internee who was chosen to be barrack chief, or "blocova," immediately commandeered the boiler as a chamber pot. Her cronies quickly snatched the other bowls for the same use.

What could the rest of us do? It seemed as though the Germans constantly sought to pit us against each other, to make us competitive, spiteful, and hateful.

In the morning, we had to be content with rinsing the bowls as well as we could before we put in our minute rations of beet-sugar or margarine. The first days our stomachs rose up at the thought of using what were actually chamber pots at night. But hunger drives, and we were so starved that we were ready to eat any food. That it had to be handled in such bowls could not be helped. During the night, many of us availed ourselves of the bowls secretly. We were allowed to go to the latrines only twice each day. How could we help it? No matter how great our need, if we went out in the middle of the night we risked being caught by the S.S., who had orders to shoot first and ask questions later.

CHAPTER IV

First Impressions

Not until two days after we were established in the koias did we receive our first morning meal — nothing except a cup of insipid, brownish liquid, pompously called "coffee." Sometimes we were given tea. To tell the truth, there was no ascertainable difference between the two beverages. They were not sweetened, yet they were our whole meal, without even a crumb, to say nothing of a crust of bread.

At noon we had soup. It was difficult to say what the ingredients were that went into the concoction. Under normal conditions, it would have been absolutely inedible. The odor was sickening. Often we could eat our portions only by holding our noses. But it was necessary to eat, and somehow we overcame our disgust. Each woman swallowed her share of the contents of the bowl in one long draught — of course, we had no spoons — like children swallowing a bitter medicine.

What went into the soup undoubtedly varied according to the season. But the flavor never changed. This did not make it any less a "surprise" soup. From it we fished buttons, tufts of hair, rags, tin cans, keys, and even mice. One fine day somebody retrieved a tiny metal sewing kit, containing thread and an assortment of needles!

In the evening we received our daily bread, a ration of six and one-half ounces. The bread was black bread with an extremely high proportion of sawdust. This was painfully irritating to our gums, which had already been made sensitive through malnutrition. The total absence of toothbrushes and dentifrices, to say nothing of the communal use of dishes, would have made any treatment useless.

Aside from the daily bread ration in the evening we received a tiny bit of beet sugar jam or a spoonful of margarine. As an exceptional favor, we sometimes had a razor-thin slice of round sausage of very doubtful origin.

Both soup and coffee were fetched in tremendous fifty-quart kettles which, contents and all, must have weighed over 150 pounds. These had to be carried by two inmates. For two women to carry such a weight through rain, snow, or ice, and often in the mud, was indeed a most difficult task. Occasionally, the carriers spilled the boiling liquid on themselves and caused serious burns. Such work would have been hard for men, and these women had had no training for manual labor and were in poor physical condition. But the German administrators enjoyed such paradoxes. They frequently placed the illiterates in the office jobs and reserved the back-breaking work for the intellectuals who were puny.

Once the kettle arrived, the soup or the coffee was distributed by the "Stubendienst," who was in charge of the service within the block. For these posts the blocova chose the largest and most brutal internees, especially those who knew how to wield a club. The Stubendiensts, dreaded dignitaries of the barrack, always had an opportunity to indulge themselves by trying out their clubs on the backs of their fellow inmates whose "conduct was not above reproach." For, seeing the kettle, some women were never able to control themselves, and fell upon the food like animals in a death struggle.

From the kettle, the liquid was poured into the twenty bowls of each barrack. Each bowl was in turn divided among the occupants of a koia. The question of who should be first caused many fights. Finally a system was established. The one given first place took the bowl under the glaring eyes of her nineteen koia neighbors. Jealously they counted every mouthful and watched the slightest movement of her Adam's apple. When she had swallowed her share of mouthfuls, the second-in-turn tore the bowl from her hands and ravenously drank her portion of the evil-smelling liquid.

What a painful sight! For no one succeeded in stifling her hunger. There was only one thing that discouraged me more, that was to see a fine, intelligent woman bend over a puddle of water and drink gluttonously to quench her thirst. She could not have been ignorant of the danger of drinking such impure liquid. But many of the deportees had already fallen so low that they were deaf to all entreaties. Death itself could come only as a deliverance.

*   *   *   *

Whenever I recall the first days at the camp, I still grow hot and cold with nameless terror. It was a terror that rose for no particular reason, but one that was constantly nourished by strange occurrences whose meaning I sought in vain. At night the glow of the flames from the chimneys of the mysterious "bakery" showed through the crevices in the walls. The shrieks of the sick or the wounded, crowded together in trucks bound for some unknown destination, grated on our nerves and made us even more miserable. Sometimes we heard revolver shots, for the S.S. guards used their guns freely. Above these noises came orders barked in overbearing voices. Nothing would let us forget our slavery. Could such conditions really exist in Europe in the twentieth century?

Our hearts went out to those we had been separated from. The camp administrators understood our longings. Two days after we arrived we were given postcards with permission to inform those we had left behind that we "were in good health." We were forced to make only one slight error. Instead of indicating that the cards were sent from Birkenau, we were to date them from Waldsee. That aroused my suspicions at once and I renounced my privilege to write.

However, most of my companions used the occasion to communicate with the outside world. Some even received replies four or five weeks later. Only in August did I understand why the German authorities had encouraged this correspondence. A new train had arrived at Auschwitz-Birkenau, and many deportees confided that the good news they had received from the camp while they were still at home had reassured them and made them neglect certain precautions that might have spared them deportation. Others stated that the cards our internees had addressed to them had given away their whereabouts to the German authorities!

So the trickery of the postcards had had a triple effect. It had deceived the families of the internees, often candidates for deportation themselves; it revealed the whereabouts of persons the Gestapo were seeking; and, thanks to the fake geographical indication, it had misled public opinion in the homelands of the internees and in foreign countries in general.

In the meantime, those who "were in good health" were penned in the "koias." The boards were nailed together clumsily and were easily wrenched apart by any excessive pressure or weight. When the third tier collapsed, it carried the second along, and crushed about sixty women. Each accident caused many wounds and fractures. We could not take care of the injured, for we had no plaster to make casts for the broken limbs. Sometimes we had eight or ten such mishaps in a single night.

When the koias were filled to the breaking point, incidents among the internees were all too frequent. During the day, the bedlam which reigned in the barrack made us hate each other. The most peaceful souls were occasionally seized with a desire to strangle their neighbors. At night the exasperation reached its height under the effects of the physical closeness. One internee, while climbing into her third tier koia, accidentally jostled an occupant of the second; a dreadful quarrel followed.

30

Another knocked over a shoe in which a crust of bread had been hidden; a violent argument resulted, including accusations of thievery.

During the night, in the midst of the crying and groaning, the inmates were constantly shouting:

"Take your feet out of my mouth!"

"Imbecile, you nearly put my eyes out!"

"Let go, you're strangling me!"

"Let me through, I beg of you . . . . I have diarrhea. I must go out." To which the Stubendienst replied, "You are insane. Go out of the barrack during the night? You'll be shot. Don't even think about it."

On one of the first nights, the blocova assembled us to witness the unseemly conduct of a deportee who was suffering from diarrhea. She had formerly been in the best society in her city. Trembling like a child caught in a naughty act, she excused herself beseechingly: "Pardon me, please. I'm terribly ashamed, but I couldn't help myself!"

Often S.S. patrols entered the barracks in the middle of the night. They never missed a chance to punish those who were responsible for "disorder," including those whose koias had fallen down. As for those who could not help themselves from falling, the Germans made them use their bare hands to clean away the traces of their own blood.

*　　　*　　　*　　　*

When I learned that our barrack chief, a Polish woman named Irka, had been in the camp for four years, I felt reassured. The only worry this big, rude woman had was that no one should miss the roll call; the rest of her authority she delegated to assistants whom she had chosen from the most brutal inmates. But no matter, the fact that Irka had been here four years showed that it was possible to exist at Birkenau. I hoped that we would not have to wait four years to leave this inferno.

31

However, when I hinted at these thoughts to Irka, she made short work of my illusions.

"You think they are going to let you live?" she jeered. "You are burying your head in the sand. All of you will be killed, except for a few rare cases, who will have, perhaps, a few months. Have you a family?"

I told her the circumstances under which I had taken my parents and my children with me, and how we had been separated from one another when we arrived at the camp.

She shrugged her shoulders with an air of indifference, and told me coldly:

"Well, I can assure you that neither your mother, your father, nor your children are in this world any more. They were liquidated and burned the same day you arrived. I lost my family the same way; and that's the case with all the old inmates here."

I listened, petrified.

"No, no, that's impossible," I mumbled. This timid protest made the block chief beside herself with impatience.

"Since you don't believe me, look for yourself!" she cried, and dragged me to the door with hysterical gestures. "You see those flames? That's the crematory oven. It would go bad with you if you let on that you knew. Call it by the name we use: the bakery. Every time a new train arrives, the ovens fall behind in their work and the dead have to wait a day or two before they are burned. Perhaps it is your family that is being burned this moment!"

When she saw that I could not even utter a single word in my desperation, a voluptuous sadness came into her voice:

"First they burn those they cannot use: the children and the old people. All those whom they put on the left side of the station are sent directly to the crematory."

I stood there as though dead. I did not cry. I was almost inert, lifeless. "Right after the arrival! When they put them aside? My Lord! I put my little boy on the left side. With my stupid love, I told the truth that he was not yet twelve years old. I wanted to spare him from the forced labor, and with this I killed him!"

I do not remember anything about the rest of that day. I lay at the bottom of my koia in a complete coma. Towards midnight someone came and shook me a long time. I opened my eyes; it was the wife of a doctor who had traveled in the same cattle car with us.

"Our husbands must not be far away," she whispered, "this evening I caught sight of Dr. X."

How impatiently I waited for the morning! I had decided that come what may, I must see my husband. I must tell him what I had learned. Perhaps he could assure me that it was only a malicious lie.

Disobeying orders and risking that an S.S. would catch me, I crept from the koia at dawn. At the entrance to the barrack, I spied a group of inmates in convict uniforms. As I approached I realized that they were inspectors. Brazenly, for by now I had no fear, I dared to ask them to help me. They refused to give any information. To be caught giving any direction would mean a sentence of twenty-five lashes.

I would not leave them. I pleaded. I begged. At last I succeeded in persuading them to pass the word for Dr. X. When he appeared he informed me that my husband was not far away. That gave me courage again. I must see him. He must know what I know. Like one obsessed, I continued to prowl and to inquire about him. Three times I was struck by German guards, for I was in a section of the camp where I should not have been; but blows did not matter, I must find him. Finally — how long it took — I located him!

Though I had lost my sensitivity after the first experiences in the camp, I still was painfully shocked when I saw my husband again. He who had always been so fastidious and correct in his grooming — Dr. Miklos Lengyel, head of a sanatorium, surgeon, splendid human being — was dirty, ragged, and emaciated. His head was shaven, and he was clad in the uniform of a

33

criminal. He, too, stared at me with unbelieving eyes. In my tattered dress, in which I was half exposed, in my striped draw-ers, and with my clipped head, I must have shocked him even worse than he did me. Certainly I did not look like the woman who had been his wife and companion in happier days.

We stood there silent, choking on our emotions. Then, in a voice that was hollow with discouragement, he spoke:

"This is where it has led us."

He did not express himself precisely, but I understood. Twen-ty years of intense effort, of toil and faith in the future, to end here, a slave of the Third Reich!

We stood near the barbed wire, and dared not linger. Any moment the guards might discover us.

As briefly as I could, I told him what the blocova had told me about the deaths of our two sons and of my parents. I spoke without expression in a tone that rang strangely in my own ears. While these words were pouring from my lips the face of my younger son, Thomas, swam before me; once he had declared that nothing bad could happen to him as long as his father and mother were with him.

I said: "I cannot believe that human beings, even Germans, would be capable of killing little children. Can you believe it? If it is true, then there is no longer any reason for living. I don't have to suffer. I have my poison. I can end it all now."

An empty silence followed my story. He did not utter a word. His haggard features did not betray any emotion. What tor-ments he had undergone I could fathom.

"I shall not tell you that you must live on in spite of every-thing," he finally murmured. "Yet perhaps you should wait."

He had understood the depths of my despair. After another pause he added hoarsely:

"Do you want to give me half of your poison? They found mine."

I was stooping to take the capsule from the lining of my boot, when he changed his mind.

"No, I don't want it. You may need it all! For me it may be easier to find another way than it will be for you, a woman."

At that moment two German guards sighted us. Savagely they pounced, and lashed us with their whips. We were chased back, each one to his own block. We did not have the time to say good-bye.

"It's all up for them," he cried, as the guards dragged him away. "We will see each other again soon! Courage!"

The next day the men were removed from the camp.

*   *   *   *

When I returned to my barrack, I met a companion who had also been on our train. His sixteen-year-old son was beside him.

"Have you seen my Thomas," I begged, hoping against hope.

"Yes, I saw him at the station," the man replied. "When he was separated from his grandmother, he was sent with two other children to the other side of the tracks, over there,"

He pointed to the right in the direction of the "bakery."

"At Block 2," the youth offered, "there is a bureau where the internees are registered and tattooed. Go there quickly! Tell them your son is twelve. Perhaps you can get him re-admitted to the camp." I hurried toward Block 2.

"Where are you running like that?" asked a German inmate. He was in a convict's uniform with a green triangle on his chest. The green triangle indicated German origin. These were the common-law murderers who often held important posts in the camp.

"I am going to try to have my son transferred to a work battalion," I told him.

"Where is he?"

"I don't know, but yesterday he was taken to the other side of the tracks."

"Then don't think about it any more," he advised with a gesture of resignation.

35

"I have to find him."

I was not crying, but I felt my eyes filling with tears.

"It is foolish," he said. "There is no use trying to find anyone here."

"I want to find my son!" I repeated obstinately.

"You would do better to worry about your own troubles," he urged. "You are still young, you can still save your own skin. If you show that you can be reasonable, you may yet receive what you need to eat and to clothe yourself. That's really all that counts."

A woman in an S.S. uniform ran up. She carried a whip with leather thongs and iron wires. I recognized Hasse, one of the feared camp commanders.

The German criminal extended a protecting hand over me.

"Don't hit her," he said. "She's a 'greenhorn.' She is looking for her son. They took him to the other side of the tracks yesterday."

The criminal winked at her and the commander seemed to be appeased. He was an attractive physical specimen, while she was a fat, ugly creature. She forgot me and gazed at the criminal intently. Hunger and lust burned in that glance. One understood these things in the camp.

He was wearing a comparatively clean convict garb and, most unusual, his head was not shaved. But then, he was not a political prisoner; he was a homicidal criminal.

The woman laughed and drew closer to him. I ran, for this time I had been spared a beating. My handsome male protector had obtained mercy for me from a female S.S. It was a topsy-turvy world which the Germans had created.

36

CHAPTER V

Roll Call and "Selections"

I already knew that there were periodic "selections" in the camp, and that at these, new victims were chosen for the crematory ovens. However, I still did not know that the roll call, too, was used to decimate the internees.

There were two roll calls daily, the first at dawn, the second at about three in the afternoon. It was at these hours that we had to be present. Before the roll call was actually called, we had to wait many hours. While waiting, no matter what the weather, we remained standing: fourteen hundred women in front of each barrack, thirty-five thousand in the whole camp, two hundred thousand in all the camps of the Birkenau-Auschwitz area. When we were accused of some infraction of the rules we had to go down on our knees and wait in the mud and dirt.

In the early dawn we shivered from the cold, especially when it rained, which was often enough. During the winter the roll call was always taken under the same conditions, whether in snow or in frost. We tried to squeeze against one another like a herd of sheep, but our warmly clothed guards were alert. Remain at attention we must and observe the required distances.

On summer afternoons the other extreme prevailed, and the sun scalded us with its flaming rays. We perspired until our filthy rags stuck to our skins. We were constantly tortured by thirst, but we dared not break ranks to seek a drop of water.

The sensation of parching thirst is inextricably entangled with all my memories of the camp, for our daily ration was hardly ever more than a quarter of a pint of water, at most two mouthfuls.

Everyone had to be present at the roll call, the sick, too. Even those who were ill with scarlet fever or pneumonia had to be there. All the stricken internees who could not stand were laid on a blanket in the first row, next to the dead. Everyone had to be present: there were absolutely no exceptions, not even for the dead.

In the beginning a few inmates tried to cheat and were absent from roll call to avoid the cold and fatigue. Their naiveté cost dearly. Sometimes an inmate stayed away because she had overslept. Such episodes were catastrophic. The missing ones had to be found, and we could not leave the rows until they were located. Even the guards lost their heads. They counted and recounted us. Others dashed here and there on their bicycles between the commander's office and the barracks. Some searched the koias. The whole camp was alerted.

The most exalted personages appeared to consider such an occurrence as an absence! The latter, chiefly S.S. women, were strange silhouettes in their large black rain capes. They looked like vultures waiting for their prey. Despite their capes and good clothing they never hesitated to seek shelter when it rained. Frequently they did not trouble to come to the roll call at all. Only the internees had to endure the inclemencies of the weather. Still, if we could catch and swallow a few drops of rain water to moisten our throats we were consoled.

Besides the ordinary roll calls, there were also special ones. A gong sounded and the fateful words, "Roll Call" were repeated in the barracks. When we heard the order — no matter where we were, in the kitchens, in the washrooms, or in the latrines — we hurried toward the assembly point as though possessed.

The camp hummed. When we got into line there was nothing to do but wait for the commanders, often on our knees, consumed by our hatred and our fears. Those who were late or who had slipped away were always discovered. The poor souls were trampled by the "kapos," who, as the officials in charge of the kommandos, rivaled each other in these "corrections," although they were internees themselves; and left the "guilty" ones with broken limbs and bloody faces.

In these special roll calls, inmates of all nationalities and social classes were thrown together. One of my neighbors was the wife of a career army officer, originally from Cracow; another was a Parisian worker. I heard the complaints of a Ukrainian peasant, the oaths of a Salonika street girl, the prayers of Czech women in pain.

"Why are you here?" we asked one other.

The replies were various:

"A German was killed in our city."

"The Gestapo pulled me from a picture theater."

"They picked me up as I was leaving church with my two children. I was not even able to notify my husband."

"I am Jewish."

"I am a Gypsy."

But the most frequent reply was still: "I haven't the slightest idea why I am here."

Most of the internees of Auschwitz resigned themselves to their fate and built up a simple philosophy: one was picked up by the Germans because she had bad luck; others were still at home at liberty because they had had good luck.

We had a few very young inmates, many practically children, in our camp. They were required to appear at the roll calls. Permitted to live a while by the Germans, these little girls, thirteen or fourteen years old, shared all the hardships of the camp life. And yet, they were privileged compared to the Jewish children of the same age, who were immediately sent to the gas chambers.

The treatment which the children received was unbelievable.

For punishment they were forced to kneel for hours at a time, sometimes with their faces turned toward the broiling sun, sometimes with stones on their heads, at other times holding a brick in each hand. No more than skin and bones, these children were dirty, starved, ragged, and barefoot. They were a pitiful sight.

Occasionally I overheard their conversations. They talked, as we did, of those things which made up our daily existence in the camp: death, hangings, the crematory ovens. They spoke calmly and realistically, just like other children of their age might speak of games and school work.

I still think about those roll calls. What reason was there for them? Why did the camp administrators concern themselves so much? Their goal was obviously to break the morale of the deportees; but also, by keeping us in the mud, the cold, or the heat, to hasten the work of extermination which was the real purpose of the camp.

*   *   *   *

The "selections" were usually made at roll calls. The women S.S., Hasse and Irma Griese, or Dr. Mengerle, Dr. Klein, and other Nazi chieftains assisted at the roll call. They chose a number of internees each time, ostensibly with a view to a would-be "transfer."

Before I ever saw them, I had heard from the older inmates that Dr. Mengerle and Irma Griese were the camp chiefs and that both were good-looking. Still, I was surprised how really handsome and, indeed, attractive they were.

Yet there was a certain wildness in Mengerle's eyes that made one uneasy. During the selections he never said a word. He merely sat whistling to himself while he pointed his thumb either to the right or to the left, thus indicating to which group the selectees were to go. Though he was making decisions that meant extermination, he was as pleasantly smug as any man could be.

40

When I laid eyes on Irma Griese, I felt sure that a woman of such beauty could not be cruel. For she was truly a blue-eyed, fair-haired "angel."

Occasionally, they picked internees for the war plants, but generally they selected only for the gas chambers. Each time they took from twenty to forty persons per barrack. When the selection was directed at the whole camp, five or six hundred internees were sent to their deaths.

Those who were chosen were immediately surrounded by Stubendiensts, who were obliged to guard them against escape, under threat of the direst punishment to themselves. The condemned men and women were led toward the main entrance. There a truck waited to transport them to the gas chambers. When the death facilities were overtaxed, they were sent to special barracks or into washrooms, to wait for hours, and sometimes days, until their turn came to be gassed. It was all done neatly and without the least feeling of compassion on the part of our masters.

In addition to the roll calls, there was also what was called a "Zahlappels," which took place inside the barrack. Suddenly, the building would be isolated and the chief S.S. physician, assisted by a woman doctor who was in charge of the deportees, herself an internee, would march in and proceed to make additional selections. The women were ordered to divest themselves completely of their rags. Then, with their arms in the air, they marched past Dr. Mengerle. What he could have seen in these wasted figures I cannot imagine. But he picked his victims. They were made to climb into a truck and were taken away, still entirely nude. Each time, this spectacle was both tragic and humiliating. Humiliating not only for the poor sacrifices, but for all humanity. For these destitute souls now being driven to the slaughterhouses were human beings — like you and me.

The Camp

When the roll call was ended, we could return to our koias or go to the latrines. I took advantage of this relative freedom to make a few "excursions" to size up the organization of this vast prison area.

The camp was divided by the "Lagerstrasse," the principal alley, which extended for about fifteen hundred feet and was flanked by seventeen barracks on either side, the even numbers on the left, the odd numbers on the right. As I indicated earlier, these buildings were originally constructed for stables. Now one was laid out for latrines, another for washrooms. Barrack No. 1 was the depot for food. No. 2 was reserved for the administration. Here was the "Schriebstube," the offices where about ten deportees worked. Here also, the home of the "Lageraelteste," the uncrowned queen of the camp. The title referred to the woman who had been there longest, although, truthfully, she was not the "dean" of the internees. Actually, the "Lageraelteste" was a young kindergarten teacher from a small Czech city. The Germans had picked her for the title, thus conferring upon her the highest authority among the deportees. The only restriction on her liberty was that she was not permitted to leave the precincts of the camp. Otherwise, she reigned as supreme mistress over the 30,000 in the women's camps, and was responsible only to the Germans. Never in her native city could she have dreamed of such authority.

The court of the Lageraelteste was composed of the "Lager-kapo," associate chief of the camp; the "Rapportschreiber," office chief; and the "Arbeitdienst," service chief. Each of these dignitaries had her own private room which, while not luxurious, was a paradise compared to the filthy holes in which the common deportees lived. The blocovas, too, had little rooms, personally and coquettishly fitted, and often furnished with ottomans and cushions. In exchange for the various services rendered to the Germans, the directresses were allowed to choose their aides from the rest of the deportees.

Frequently, ironic situations resulted. One blocova, formerly maid-of-all-work, selected her erstwhile mistress as her personal servant. The latter brushed the shoes and mended the tatters of her ex-maid.

A lesser hierarchy reigned in our own barrack. The blocova was at the top. She was assisted by her "Vertreterin," or representative; and her "Schreiberin," or secretary, whose particular duty it was to edit the roll call and reports; by the doctor (whose function was wholly illusory, since there were no medicines); and by the nurses and "stubendiensten," numbering six or eight.

Camp policewomen were also selected from the inmates. These wore blue work outfits. Their principal duty was to drive off all who approached too close to the barbed wire, whether to communicate with the inmates in other enclosures, or for any other matters. When it rained they wrapped themselves in blankets, which made them look like ghosts, especially during the night. We also had a few women firemen, garbage collectors, and corpse-gatherers.

The kitchen staff consisted of about four hundred women. Part of barrack No. 2 was reserved for them; they, too, were privileged persons. They did not eat the ordinary food, except as part of punishments. For themselves they prepared special suppers. For their personal use they commandeered much of the food intended for the camp, notably the potatoes, of which we never saw a speck. They also helped themselves generously to the preserves and the margarine, not only for their own consumption but also for a medium of exchange. With this currency they were able to procure indispensable clothing. The term "Musulmans," used to describe the walking skeletons so numerous in Auschwitz, could never be applied to them.

However, these kitchen girls often handled difficult assignments. Some unloaded trucks of wood, coal, and potatoes. Others cleaned all day long or performed real convict work with their feet almost always in water. Their hands became deformed, and their feet were covered with eczema. When they were caught stealing they were compelled to run within the camp for hours at a time while carrying heavy stones in either hand. A three-inch strip of hair was clipped from the middle of their heads. The Germans called this "sport."

It would be difficult to say which of the internees were treated worst. Most of us, whether political, racial, or criminal prisoners, were reduced to existence on the animal level. But the Jews and the Russians were treated cruelly. On the other hand, the German internees, whether common-law criminals, perverts, or political prisoners, benefited from certain privileges. They provided large numbers of the camp functionaries; and, no matter what their duties, were never chosen in the dreaded "selection."

*   *   *   *

Two barracks had been turned into washrooms. Across each building two metal pipes ran, carrying water to the taps, which were placed about forty inches apart. Beneath the pipes was a sort of trough intended to catch the water. Most of the time there was no water at all.

The water was turned on once or twice a day and for about an hour or two we were theoretically free to wash. The "washroom" was supposed to be the place where we cleaned ourselves. There we had to wash, rinse our mouths, and comb our hair.

44

Yet it was practically impossible to do that, even when there was water.

Every day a dense crowd swarmed outside the building. This herd of dirty, evil-smelling women inspired a profound disgust in their companions and even in themselves. However, we did not congregate with any intention of washing but rather in the hope that we would be able to quench our constant thirst. What was the point of going there to clean up when we had no soap, no toothbrushes, and no combs?

Besides, precious water meant something to drink. Our water ration was absurdly minute. Tortured by thirst we never missed a chance to exchange our meager pittances of bread or margarine for a half pint of water. Better to endure hunger than that hell-fire that was constantly gnawing at our gullets. The water that came through the rusted washroom pipes smelled evilly. It had a very suspicious color and was hardly fit to drink. But it was no less joy to swallow a few drops, even though we might pay for the temporary relief with an attack of dysentery or some other disease. This water was better than the rain which stagnated in the puddles; some internees lapped this slop like dogs, and died.

The washroom would have made a fine field for a moralist's observations. Sometimes an internee was able to clean up after a fashion, despite all handicaps. If she did, it usually went badly with her. Most of the time she would not be able to find her clothing where she had left it, for it would have been stolen. In the camp, thievery had become a science, an art. The thief knew that her victims would have to go out nude and be subjected to horrible beatings by the Germans. Women who had been mothers of honest families, who formerly would not have taken a hairpin, became utterly hardened thieves and never suffered the slightest feeling of remorse.

What prices we paid for a half pint of water! Yet, sometimes, at the very moment one raised the dearly acquired liquid to her lips, another internee tore the glass away. What could anyone do? The unwritten laws of the camp did not sanction such aggression. That did not soothe the victims in this jungle. Perhaps the Germans wanted to infect us with their own Nazi morals. In most cases, they succeeded.

*　　　*　　　*　　　*

Two huts were provided for the latrines. Each latrine consisted of a paved ditch about a yard deep. On top, two cement chests, like enormous boxes, about 30 inches high, were mounted. Each chest contained two holes to meet the needs of our vast population. There were about 300 of these in the camp.

Each day they had to be cleaned. For such a task, intellectuals — doctors or teachers — were usually preferred by our masters.

During the "free" hours, access to these latrines was no easier than to the washrooms. We had to jostle each other to get in and once inside, we had to wait our turns. If one had to hurry she exposed herself to serious penalties. Still, haste was hardly possible as long as great numbers of internees suffered from chronic enteritis. This malady was responsible for the uncleanliness around the latrines. The sick who were incapable of holding back relieved themselves near the barracks. If they were discovered their overseers beat them savagely. A total lack of paper was another difficulty that made personal hygiene impossible, to say nothing of the cleanliness of the latrines.

Frequently, inmates of both sexes found themselves side by side in the washrooms and latrines. Many men worked on road repairs and other tasks in the women's camps. When the washrooms were not crowded, they became "salons," especially at noon. Some internees even brought their "lunches." Here news was exchanged, and most of the black market dealings took place.

Another spot where we gathered was the garbage corner, for many precious objects could be found there.

46

I badly needed a waistband to hold up my drawers. At the garbage dump, by a wonderful stroke of luck, I found three fragments of twine which could be pieced together for the purpose. I also found a flat piece of wood, which I could sharpen into a knife.

The same day fortune smiled on me again. One of my koia companions gave me a royal gift: two fragments of rag. It took no study to decide what I would do with them. One would serve me as a toothbrush, the other as a handkerchief. I had a bad cold and, despite every effort, I was never to become dexterous in the art of blowing my nose with my fingers. I confess I envied my companions who could do so.

I had no pockets, so I attached the two hygienic accessories to my new waistband, near the wooden knife. These new acquisitions filled me with pride. I felt that I had become a rich woman in the camp.

CHAPTER VII

A Proposal in Auschwitz

Three weeks after I arrived at Auschwitz, I still could not believe it. I lived as in a dream, waiting for someone to awaken me.

The inmates cried and quarreled and hurt one another. Their babbling sounded vaguely like the noise of a pack of animals. From my koia I looked out into the barrack as through a veil, unhappy and apathetic.

Through this concert of misery, I suddenly heard a kindly human voice. I roused myself and glanced at the top of the koia. A handsome blue-eyed man in a striped uniform leaned down from the third tier. I was surprised to see a man. This was a women's barrack.

Since morning he had been repairing the bunks, but I had been so lethargic that I had not heard him hammering. He looked at me and said, "Chin up! What's the matter with you?"

I stared but did not answer. So he climbed down. I saw that he was tall. His eyes were a clear, sparkling blue; and although, of course, his hair had been clipped, the stubble was brown. He was smiling. That caught my attention. How could a man smile in this camp? I had found somebody who had not succumbed to the spiritual degradation.

He continued to talk and drew me into a conversation. I learned that he was Polish and that he had been in prison camps for four years, ever since the fall of Warsaw. Laughingly, he told me that he was a carpenter. Sometimes he cleaned the latrines or worked with the road gang.

Each day thereafter he came to repair the beds. We talked and became friends. After a while I waited eagerly for his visits. I was not expecting him as a man. His was the only human-sounding voice I had heard in the camp.

The workers were allowed a recess of one hour, usually around 11 A. M., from the position of the sun. One day he told me to follow him when he left. I was indeed grateful for the invitation and went with him. Up to that time it had never occurred to me that I might leave the barrack for a moment.

I followed him closely. Finally, we reached a clearing where workers were cooking food over a fire. To my astonishment, my friend, whose name was Tadek, produced two potatoes, a rare treasure, and set them to boil in a pot. I followed his every motion with my eyes.

It was like a childhood excursion. Tadek gave me one potato. He sat down opposite me and began to devour the other. This was the first scrap of food I could keep in my stomach. Up to that moment, I had thrown up every mouthful I had swallowed in the camp.

Tadek had another surprise. He gave me a shawl. "You must wrap this around your head. It must be a terrible thing for a woman to go around without any hair," he said.

I was overcome. I wanted to thank him, but I could not trust myself to open my mouth for fear that I should cry.

"Every day you will share my potatoes," he continued. "And perhaps I shall be able to 'organize' some other food, and a little clothing, too."

He stood close to me. Then, as though talking to himself, he said, "It's a strange thing, even though you have no hair and are dressed in rags, there is something very desirable about you."

I felt his arm around my waist. His other hand touched me and began to fondle my breast.

My world fell to pieces again. I had already told him what

49

had happened to me — that I had lost my family! Could he not understand how I felt? I wanted to be friends with the human being in him, not with his lust.

I learned afterwards that his was the finest style of love-making in Auschwitz. The ordinary approach was much more crude and to the point. I stood there silently, tears running down my cheeks.

He was flustered. "Don't yell," he grumbled. "If you don't want it now, I shall wait. If you change your mind, let me know. You will see me at work."

The gong sounded, and he turned away.

For a parting word, Tadek added, "In the meantime, we can talk, but you get no food! I haven't much, and with the little I do have, I must get my women. In this misery and excitement we need them more than in normal life. Women are cheap enough, but it is almost impossible to find a place where we can be safe. The Germans watch constantly, and if we are caught we pay with our lives."

Then he was ashamed. "You do not understand. I am always cold and hungry. All the time they beat me, and I never know when I am going to be shot. You are still a novice; you will change. In a few weeks you will understand."

Every day Tadek entered our barrack and brought a package of food — not for me — for another woman. Whenever he passed he offered me the food. Sometimes we did not even exchange a word. He held out the package and I turned my head. Day after day I grew thinner, and he smiled more sarcastically as I refused his offerings. After a few weeks I could hardly walk, and frequently fainted during the roll call. But I had made up my mind not to give in.

Yet I knew I could not go on this way.

I decided to go to the washroom where I had heard that the men, congregating during the rest hour, occasionally shared their food with the women. I prayed that I would find at least one person who would have pity for me.

When I arrived, I saw the prisoners posted to watch for the guards. They pretended that they were working, for it was strictly against the rules for women to enter when the men were there.

The scene inside was demoralizing. In the back of the filthy barrack men were drinking soup from dirty tin cans they had retrieved from the garbage dump.

The place was crowded. Men and women huddled together in every corner of the room. Couples pressed against one another, talking. Others sat against the walls in close embrace. A few were engaged in black market transactions. The smell of the unwashed bodies mingled with the stale odors of mouldy food and the general dampness. The air was unendurable.

In another part of the camp another scene was being enacted. A new transport had just arrived; and the screams of the women and children, being separated in the first selection as they disembarked from the trains, rose above the conversation in the washroom. Flames from the crematory chimneys belched toward the sky.

Hardly had I stepped across this threshold than I wanted to run. But I could not. At my stomach tore a gnawing pain that was more than simple hunger.

An elderly man leaned against the wall in a corner eating from a tin can. He was horrible to look at, but perhaps that was why I felt that I could trust him. He was fifty-five or sixty years old. Not a tooth remained in his mouth. His face was pock-marked and covered with scars. On his head were steatoma. And, as though fate had not played enough tricks on him, he had only one eye.

In the brownish liquid in his tin floated two small potatoes. Potatoes! I stared at them greedily as he gnawed. But he could only eat the outside. The insides were still raw and too hard for his toothless gums. What he could not eat, he dropped back into the tin. He drank the brownish "soup," and the potatoes remained. He glanced around him. Was he seeking

51

someone with whom to share this princely gift? He saw me glaring hungrily. With a smile that was so distorted and horrible that I felt I would go mad, he offered me the remainder of his lunch. I clutched at his gift and began to feed. Suddenly, a woman leaped at me and snatched the potatoes from my hand. "You dirty pig!" she shrieked at the old man. "You gave the food away to somebody else?"

"Go to hell!" he replied. "I do what I please. She is younger than you."

He flung the woman from me, threw her to the ground, and kicked her. The woman's sobbing attracted the other occupants of the washroom. All of them, even the busy lovers, crowded around. My face flamed.

Suddenly Tadek approached. "I'm surprised to see you here, Your Highness," he smiled sarcastically. "You held out very long. This will be better than half-eaten potatoes." He offered me the usual package. We looked at each other. How I hated him! I seized his package and with all my strength I hurled it into his face. Then I ran. To this day, I cannot remember how I got back.

For some time after this last meeting I had no contact with Tadek. However, I did see Lilli, the woman to whom he now brought his food parcels. When, later, I worked at the infirmary my rival became a regular visitor. I spent my bread ration to buy a rare medicine for her on the black market. The medicine was to combat syphilis.

CHAPTER VIII

I Am Condemned to Death

Some days stretched endlessly. The enforced idleness nearly drove us mad. Our only activity came at the roll calls.

I had become as thin as a skeleton; a prey to fever and fits of coughing. I was always getting chills. I had one at the beginning of summer when it was raining and the weather was cool. One day, feeling particularly ill, I covered my back with a piece of shabby wool a neighbor had lent me. Encouraged by my example, Magda, one of my friends who had a sore throat, wrapped a rag around her throat. We hoped that the "Fuehrerin," the hateful Hasse, wouldn't notice anything and that we would be able to snatch off the extra garments before she neared us.

Even this did not work out as we had hoped. Hasse immediately observed the changes in our dress. A serious infringement of discipline. She thrashed us roundly; and then, apparently still vengeful, designated us for the "selection." Thus she condemned us to death for an unfortunate peccadillo. On that particular day the selected ones included a few dozen from our barrack. The "Stubendiensts" corralled us over to the camp exit. We were told to stay there and wait. The truck which was to take us to the gas chamber had not yet arrived.

For many days, selections, the gas chamber, and the crematory oven had been the subjects of long arguments in our barrack. My companions believed that all the stories were largely fantastic rumors and nothing more.

53

I already knew that a selection meant the gas chamber. Many others had also learned this secret, but it was as difficult to get the majority to understand as it is difficult to make the reader fathom the conditions under which we existed. We were no more than a few hundred yards from the so-called "bakery," and could smell the sweetish odor that wafted from it.

They burned people in this "bakery." Yet, after months of internment there were still people in the camp who could not believe that it was possible.

Why did they refuse to accept the truth? I asked myself that many times. Perhaps they doubted because they did not want to believe. Even at the moment when they were being pushed into the gas chamber, many refused to believe. Magda was such an optimist.

Often I was in a dilemma. What attitude should I take toward those who refused to believe that there were gas chambers and crematories? Should I have let them continue to think that the whole story was idle gossip, a cunning instrument in the hands of the sadistic blocovas when they wanted to frighten us? Was it not my duty to enlighten my fellow-sufferers? If I did not convince them of the cruel truth, they might offer them-selves at the next selection.

As we waited for the truck, the Stubendiensts and the German internees joined hands and formed a circle around us. I muttered to Magda about trying to get out of this ring. She shook her head and replied, "No, the camp is so terrible that no matter where they take us, it must be an improvement. I shall not escape."

"You fool," I scolded her. "We were selected for punishment. Obviously, wherever they send us will be worse. Will you come with me?"

"No!"

"Then I shall try to break out alone."

But that was more easily said than done. No sooner had I outlined a plan for escape then several of the "selectionees" cried, "Stubendienst! Somebody is trying to get away."

Why did they betray me? True, they did not know that they were going to their deaths, but they knew that the selections were not carried out to improve their lots. However, they begrudged anyone who might save himself from the common fate, not having the courage to risk any action themselves.

I was forced to remain in the ranks, trembling. I tried to slip away as far as possible from my neighbors in front. While I was engaged in these maneuvers, the gas-chamber truck arrived. Instinctively, the group backed away. Suddenly, by a miracle of miracles, I spied a stick lying on the ground. In Auschwitz a stick was a symbol of power and authority. I picked up the stick and mingled with a group of stubendiensts from another barrack. Then I dashed off at top speed toward the kitchens. Magda, who had changed her mind in the meantime, followed me. As always, a crowd of internees loitered before the kitchens. With a businesslike air, I began to put the dishes in order. Afterward I offered help to the soup-pot carriers, and thus proceeded from barrack to barrack until I succeeded in reaching my own. Magda, who had done exactly as I did, disappeared into another block. Not without difficulty, I changed clothing with another deportee and hid in my koia.

I was careful not to go out until the next roll call. One or two internees were astonished to see me, but I calmly explained that they must have confused me with someone else. I had not been selected at all.

The clothing exchange aroused some suspicion. I was sure that Hasse would not recognize me from among the 40,000 other inmates. Still, I felt that it would be better not to let her see me in my old dress.

But if my calm stilled most of my companions, it did not fool Irka, the blocova. The next day, I was awakened at dawn by the stubendienst who was the blocova's personal servant.

"Irka says she wants your boots immediately, or else she will denounce you to Hasse."

55

I tried to protest. "I am sick, I have a fever. It's raining and I have absolutely nothing else to put on my feet."

"Don't worry so much," replied the faithful stubendienst, "Irka will give you a pair of shoes."

The deal was closed!

In the morning I received two different kinds of shoes, both for the left foot, both in shreds and almost entirely soleless.

But I dared not complain. I had not made such a bad bargain. I was still among the living.

CHAPTER IX

The Infirmary

For weeks there were no facilities for the care of the sick. No hospital for health services had been organized and no pharmaceutical products were available. One day we were told that we were finally to have an infirmary. But here again they used a magnificent word to describe a piddling reality.

I became a member of the infirmary staff. How I happened to be chosen was another story. A short time after my arrival I plucked up my courage to ask Dr. Klein, the chief S.S. doctor of the camp, to allow me to do something to relieve the sufferings of my companions. He rebuked me sharply, for it was forbidden to address an S.S. doctor without authorization. The next day, however, he sought me out and declared that henceforth I would be in charge of liaison with the doctors of the different barracks. He lost a lot of precious time listening to their reports in the course of his rounds and needed help.

Soon a new order was issued. All internees with any knowledge of medical practice should make themselves known. Many volunteered. As I was not without experience, I was ordered into infirmary work.

Barrack No. 15, probably the most dilapidated in the camp, was to house the new service. The rain leaked through the roof and the walls had enormous, gaping holes. To the right and to the left of the entrance were two small rooms. One was designated the "infirmary" and the other the "pharmacy." A few weeks later, a "hospital" was installed at the other end of the barrack, and we were able to assemble four or five hundred patients.

For a long time, however, we had only the two small rooms. The only light came from the corridor; there was no running water, and the wooden floor was difficult to keep clean, though we washed it twice a day with cold water. Without boiling water and disinfectants, we could not scrub away the traces of blood and pus in the crevices.

The furniture of our infirmary consisted of a pharmacy closet without shelves, a shaky examination table which we had to prop up with bricks, and a long table which we covered with a sheet to hold our instruments. We had little else, and whatever we did have was in poor condition.

Whenever we had to use anything we were confronted with the same problem: should we use the unsterilized instruments or do without them? For example, after treating a boil or an anthrax, we might have to treat an abscess of lesser gravity with the same instruments. We knew that we were exposing our patient to infection. What could we do? It was a miracle that we never had a serious infection because of this situation. Sometimes we wondered whether our experience did not refute all medical theories on sterilization.

The internees in our camp totaled from thirty to forty thousand. And the entire personnel in our infirmary consisted of five women! Needless to say, we were swamped with work.

We rose at four in the morning. The consultations began at five. The sick, of whom there were often as many as fifteen hundred in a day, had to wait their turns by rows of five. It was pitiful to behold these columns of ailing women, scantily clad, standing humbly in the rain, snow, or frost. Often when their last strength ebbed they fainted like so many tenpins falling.

The consultations continued without a respite from daybreak until three in the afternoon, when we paused for our rest period. We devoted this time to our soup, if there was any left; and to clean up the floor and the instruments. We operated as late as eight in the evening. Sometimes we had accouchements during the night. We were literally crushed by the burden of the work. Confined to the one hut, which was completely without fresh air, without exercise, and sufficient rest we could not look forward to any relief.

Although we lacked everything, even bandages, we proceeded with fervor, spurred on by our consciousness of the great responsibility. When we felt we were at the end of our resistance we sprinkled our faces and necks with a few drops of precious water. We had to sacrifice these few drops to keep going. But the never-ending effort exhausted us. When there were several accouchements in succession and we had to spend sleepless nights, we became so fatigued that we staggered about as though intoxicated. However, we had an infirmary; and we were doing good, useful work.

I shall always remember the joy I felt after, having completed my first day's work at the infirmary, I was finally free to go to bed. For the first time in many weeks, we no longer had to sleep in the indescribable promiscuity of the koia, and its filth, lice, and stench. There were only five women workers in this relatively vast room.

Before retiring, we indulged in the luxury of a good wash, thanks to our new basin. This utensil leaked in two places and could be used only if the hole were stopped with bits of bread, but what did that matter? It was a real basin, on a real stand. It contained real water; even a bit of soap, that supreme luxury. What they called soap here was merely sticky paste of doubtful origin and with a sickening odor; but it did lather, if somewhat indifferently.

We five had two blankets. One we spread over the floor, which we had not been able to clean, and the other we used to cover us. By normal standards we were not very comfortable. It rained the first night, and the wind blew in through the cracks in the boards. The dilapidated roof let the rain come in, and many times we had to move from the puddles. However, after the barrack, this was paradise.

From one day to the next, our living conditions improved. We had a certain degree of independence, relative to be sure; but we could talk among ourselves and were free to go to the latrine when necessary. People who have never been deprived of these small liberties cannot imagine how precious they can be.

Yet our clothing situation remained the same. While taking care of the sick we wore the same rags which served as our night shirts, gowns, and what not. But the sick were scarcely aware of it, since all were dressed like scarecrows unless they were in convict uniform.

In the beginning the infirmary personnel slept in the consultation room on the floor. Imagine our joy when, one day, we were given "an apartment." True, it was the old urinal in Barrack No. 12, but it was to be our own. The room was so small that it could barely hold two narrow camp beds. Therefore, we adopted the system of beds in tiers, as in the barracks. Three tiers made six bunks. It was like a dream. The little dormitory was henceforth our private domicile. There we were at home. Many evenings were spent in discussion, pondering the chances for liberation and endlessly analyzing the latest developments in the war, as we understood them. On rare occasions, a German newspaper was smuggled in and for long hours we examined each word, seeking a speck of truth in all the lies.

Often we reminisced, speaking of the ones who were dear to us or simply discussing the tormenting problems of the day, such as should we or should we not condemn the newborn to death in order to save the poor mothers. We even recited poetry to lull ourselves into a calm state of mind to forget, to escape the frightful present.

The results achieved at our infirmary were far from brilliant.

60

The deplorable conditions in the camp caused the number of sick to increase. However, our masters would not augment our personnel. Five women were enough. We could have given part of our medicaments and bandages to the doctors residing in the other barracks, but the Germans would not allow us to do that.

Naturally, we could not take care of all the patients; and many cases were aggravated through neglect: for example, when we had to care for gangrenous wounds. The infections gave off a putrid odor and maggots multiplied rapidly in them. We used a tremendous syringe and disinfected them with a solution of potassium permanganate. But we had to repeat the operation ten or twelve times and our water was exhausted. So as a result, other patients, still waiting, suffered.

The situation eased somewhat when the hospital was installed at the other end of the barrack. This space was reserved for cases requiring surgery, but, in a pinch, all kinds of infections were treated. The hospital held from four to five hundred patients, and was always filled. Moreover, it was difficult to gain admission, so those who were ill frequently had to wait days before being hospitalized. Upon their arrival here, they had to abandon all their effects in exchange for a worthless shirt. They still had to sleep in koias on scanty straw mattresses but with only one blanket for four people. Of course, there could be no question of real scientific isolation.

Still, the most tragic danger for the sick was the menace of the "selection," which threatened them more than it did the internees in good health. The selection meant a trip to the gas chamber or an injection of phenol in the heart. I first learned about the phenol from Dr. Pasche, an underground member. When the Germans launched their mass selections, it was dangerous to be in the hospital. We therefore encouraged those who were not too ill to stay in their barracks. But, especially in the beginning, the internees refused to believe that hospitalization might be used against them to expedite their journey to the gas chamber. They imagined, naively, that the choices made at the hospital and at the roll calls were for transfers to other camps, and that the sick were sent to a central hospital.

Before the infirmary was established and I was assigned to the service of Dr. Klein, I one day told my fellow internees that they should avoid even the appearance of illness. Later that same day I had to accompany Dr. Klein on his rounds. This man was different from the other S.S. He never shouted, and had rather nice manners. One of the sick women remarked to him, "We appreciate your kindness, Herr Oberarzt," and she went on to say that some people in the camp pretended that the sick were sent to the gas chamber.

Dr. Klein simulated surprise. With a smile he said, "You don't have to believe all the silly things they say around here. Who spread this rumor?"

I trembled. Only this morning I had told this poor creature the truth. Fortunately, the blocova came to my rescue. She wrinkled her eyebrows and literally crushed the prattler with an icy stare.

The sick woman understood that she had spoken out of turn and beat a hasty retreat. "Oh, I don't know anything about it," she mumbled. "They say all sorts of things around here."

In another camp hospital, Section B-3, there were about six thousand deportees in August, 1944, considerably fewer than our thirty-five thousand. There they had isolated rooms for the contagious cases. Characteristic of the irrational way in which the camps were organized, this, the smaller section, had an infirmary ten times as large as ours, with fifteen doctors on service. However, the hygienic conditions there were even more deplorable, for there were no latrines at all, only wooden chests in the open air, where the female inmates were under the eyes of the S.S. and the male deportees.

Whenever we had contagious cases we had to take them to that section hospital. This troubled us. If we kept the contagious cases, we risked spreading the disease. But once they were in the hospital the sick women ran the risk of being selected. Yet the rule was strict, and we exposed ourselves to dangerous punishment if we kept the contagious cases. Besides, Dr. Mengerle made frequent tours and checked up. Needless to say, we infringed upon the rules as often as possible.

The transfer of the contagious cases made a pitiful spectacle as, burning with fever and covered with their blankets, they walked along the "Lagerstrasse." The other inmates avoided them as though they were lepers. Some of the unfortunates were confined in the "Durchgangszimmer" (passageway), a room nine by twelve feet, where the sick had to lie on the bare ground. This was a real antechamber of death.

Those who entered this gateway to destruction were at once removed from the lists of effectives and were thenceforth given nothing to eat. So they had only the final journey to look forward to. At last the "Red Cross" trucks would come and the sick would be packed into them like sardines. Protests were useless. They were piled one on top of another. The German responsible for the shipment locked the door and took his place beside the driver. The truck started its trip to the gas chamber. That was why we dreaded taking contagious cases to the "hospital."

The system of administration was completely without logic. It was stupefying to see how little the orders which followed one another had in common. This was only partly due to negligence. The Germans apparently sought also to baffle the internees, thus minimizing the danger of revolt. The same methods prevailed with the selections. For a while one category of sick would automatically be selected. Then one day it would all change, and those who had the same affliction, say diphtheria, would be put under treatment in an isolated room under the care of deportee doctors.

Most of the time it was hazardous to have scarlet fever; yet, occasionally, those who had this disease were taken care of, and some were even cured. They were sent back to their old barracks, and their example convinced the others that scarlet fever could not condemn one to the gas chamber. Soon, thereafter, the policy would change again. How could any one know what, therefore, to believe?

Be that as it may, only in very rare cases did our sick ever return from the section hospital, and these had never moved through the Durchgangszimmer, so that they were not well informed of the conditions. That "hospital" remained a horror for all of us. It was surrounded by mystery and filled with danger and death.

*   *   *   *

At that hospital I once witnessed a particularly moving scene. Eva Weiss, one of the nurses, a young, pretty Jewish girl from Hungary, had caught scarlet fever while caring for her patients. On the day she discovered that she had it, the Germans had just ceased to tolerate it. Since the diagnosis had been made by a German doctor the nurse knew that her departure for the gas chamber was certain. She knew that soon the fake ambulance would come to get her, and all the other sick who had been selected.

Those who suspected the truth were in the depths of despair. The room resounded with groans and lamentations.

"I assure you that there is nothing to be alarmed about!" said Eva Weiss, who also came from Cluj. "You are imagining terrifying things. Actually, this is what is going to happen. We shall be transferred to a larger hospital where they will take much better care of us than they do here. I can even tell you where this hospital is located. It is in the old folks' and the children's camp. The nurses there are all old women. Perhaps some of us will find our mothers. After all, we should realize how fortunate we are."

"A nurse," thought the sick, "must be well informed." And her words reassured them.

Before the door of the ambulance closed, the other nurses said their last good-bye to Eva, their comrade. This young heroine, with her cool courage, had spared her unfortunate companions the usual torturing anxieties. What she herself experienced on her way to death one had best not even think of.

*   *   *   *

Of course I saw hundreds of tragic cases. No book can be written that could include them all. But one moved me especially.

A young Greek girl was brought to us from a neighboring barrack. Though worn out by illness and as thin as a skeleton, she was still very beautiful. She would not answer any of our questions and behaved like a mute.

We specialized mostly in surgery and could not understand why she had been sent to us. Her medical card indicated no need for surgery.

We placed her under observation. Soon we discovered that an error had been made. The young Greek girl should have been sent to the section for the mentally ill. She sat nearly all the time, imitating the precision-like gestures of a spinning-mill worker. From time to time, as if worn out by her work, she lost consciousness. Nor could she be revived for an hour or two. Then she shook her head, opened her eyes, and threw her arms up, as though to shield her head from a beating.

A day later, we found her dead. During the night she had emptied her straw mattress to "spin" the straw. She had also torn her blouse into tiny shreds to make more raw material for her imaginary spindle. I have seen many dead, but few faces upset me as much as that of the young Greek girl. She had probably been employed somewhere as a forced laborer in a spinning mill. Her efforts had brought her nothing but beatings. She succumbed, and the desperate animal fear had finally destroyed the equilibrium of her mind.

CHAPTER X

A New Reason for Living

Occasionally, men came to our infirmary. These were usually internees employed in the women's camps as laborers. When they returned to their places in the evening, their infirmaries were closed. We could not refuse to treat them, although it was strictly *verboten* by the Germans. But their injuries had resulted from accidents at work.

Among these ailing men was an elderly Frenchman, whom I shall call "L." A bad wound on his foot made him a regular visitor to the infirmary.

L. was a charming person, and we welcomed him joyfully. Each time he brought comforting news on the military and political situation in Europe. While we nursed his hurts, he soothed our troubled spirits.

L. was almost the only source of world news we had. At least he gave factual information, not fantastic rumors. From the attitude of our jailers it was impossible to draw any conclusions, for they seemed to regard the camp as a permanent institution. Seen from Auschwitz-Birkenau, the bloody war was far away and almost unreal. Indeed, we had no war experiences except infrequent air raid alarms. When the latter sounded, the brave S.S. fled from the camp at full speed to hide in the forests, pausing only to return us to our camps. They carefully locked all the gates: the inmates were exposed to the danger of the expected bombs, while the S.S. sought shelter.

Because I was passing through a serious nervous depression the news that L. brought was a real booster to my morale. In material things my situation had improved since I had started to work at the infirmary. Yet my life seemed a frightful burden. I had lost my parents and my children, and I had no word of my husband, the only person whose existence could keep me in the land of the living. I was mentally ripe for suicide. My companions saw that I was wasting away before their eyes.

One day L. took me aside. "You have no right to throw away your life," he scolded. "If this existence has no more attraction for you personally, you must go on if only to try to relieve the sufferings of the others around you. Your position is perfect for rendering service in many ways."

He gave me a penetrating glance. "Obviously," he continued, "this will not be without danger. But isn't danger our daily bread here? The essential thing is to have a goal, a purpose."

It was my turn to look squarely into his eyes. "I place myself at your service," I returned. "What must I do?"

"You can do two things for us," he replied. "First, you can spread carefully all the news that I give you. This is of the utmost importance to maintain the morale of our internees. Do you agree?"

The dissemination of "false news" was forbidden by the Germans on pain of death. But what was death? I did not even think of it.

"Second," he went on, "your job makes you ideal to serve as a post office. People will bring you letters and parcels. You will deliver them according to the instructions you are given. And not a word to anyone, not even to your best friends. For if you are ever caught, you will be questioned, and we do not want there to be any witnesses against you. Not everybody can stand torture! Do you think you would be strong enough to take their torture?"

I was silent. Were there more sufferings one could undergo? "I could try to be strong."

He reflected, then added: "Still another thing. We must observe everything that goes on here. Later we shall write down all that we have seen. When the war is over the world must know about this. It must know the truth."

From that moment on I had a new reason for living. I was a member of the resistance movement.

After that interview I had the opportunity to meet others in our "underground." We limited our relations to our work and did not seek to learn one another's names. Caution made this mandatory so that we could avoid betraying each other should we be arrested and tortured.

Through these new contacts, I finally learned the minutest details about the gas chamber and the crematories.

*   *   *   *

In the beginning, those who were condemned to death at Birkenau were either shot in the forest of Braezinsky or gassed at the infamous white house in the camp. The corpses were incinerated in a "deathpit." After 1941 four crematory ovens were put into service and the "output" of this immense extermination plant was augmented vastly.

At first, Jews and non-Jews were sent to the crematory equally, without favor. After June, 1943, the gas chamber and the crematory ovens were reserved exclusively for Jews and Gypsies. Except for reprisal or by error, Aryans were not sent there. But generally, Aryans were executed by shooting, hanging, or by poison injections.

Of the four crematory units at Birkenau, two were huge and consumed enormous numbers of bodies. The other two were smaller. Each unit consisted of an oven, a vast hall, and a gas chamber.

Above each rose a high chimney, which was usually fed by nine fires. The four ovens of Birkenau were heated by a total of thirty fires. Each oven had large openings. That is, there

68

were 120 openings, into each of which three corpses could be placed at one time. That meant they could dispose of 360 corpses per operation. That was only the beginning of the Nazi "Production Schedule."

Three hundred and sixty corpses every half hour, which was all the time it took to reduce human flesh to ashes, made 720 per hour, or 17,280 corpses per twenty-four hour shift. And the ovens, with murderous efficiency, functioned day and night.

However, one must also reckon the death pits, which could destroy another 8,000 cadavers a day. In round numbers, about 24,000 corpses were handled each day. An admirable production record — one that speaks well for German industry.

Even while in camp I obtained very detailed statistics on the number of convoys which arrived at Auschwitz-Birkenau in 1942 and 1943. Today, the Allies know the exact number of such arrivals, for these figures were attested to many times in the course of the war criminals' trials. I shall cite only a few examples.

In February, 1943, two or three trains arrived at Birkenau every day. Each was thirty to fifty cars long. These transports included a large proportion of Jews, but also numbers of other enemies of the Nazi regime — political prisoners of all nationalities, ordinary criminals, and a considerable number of Russian prisoners-of-war. However, the supreme specialty of Auschwitz-Birkenau was the extermination of the Jews of Europe, the undesirable element par excellence, according to Nazi doctrine. Hundreds of thousands of Israelites were burned in the crematory ovens.

Sometimes the ovens were so overtaxed that they could not do all the work even on the twenty-four hour a day shift. The Germans then had to burn the corpses in the "death pits." These were trenches about sixty yards long and about four yards wide. They were provided with a cunning system of ditches to drain off the human fat.

There was also a time when the trains came in even greater

69

numbers. In 1943, forty-seven thousand Greek Jews were brought to Birkenau. Thirty-nine thousand were executed immediately. The others were interned, but they died like flies, unable to adapt themselves to the climate. Indeed, the Greeks and the Italians, probably because they were most poorly nourished before they came, bore up the poorest under the cold and the privations. In 1944 came the turn of the Hungarian Jews, and more than a half million of them were exterminated.

I have the figures only for the months of May, June and July, 1944. Dr. Pasche, a French doctor of the Sonderkommando, in the crematory, who was in a position to gather statistics on the rate of the extermination, provided me with these:

May, 1944	360,000
June, 1944	512,000
From the 1st to the 26th of July, 1944	442,000
	1,314,000

In less than a quarter of a year the Germans had "liquidated" more than 1,300,000 persons at Auschwitz-Birkenau!

*   *   *   *

I had ample opportunity to witness the arrival of new trainloads of deportees. One day, in the company of three other internees, I was sent out for blankets for the infirmary.

When we reached the station, a transport had just steamed in. The cattle cars were being emptied of the bruised and starved human beings who had traveled together, about one hundred packed together into each car. From this vast, miserable assembly piteous cries rose in every language of Europe; in French, Rumanian, Polish, Czech, Dutch, Greek, Spanish, Italian; who knows how many more?

"Water! Water! Something to drink!"

When I had arrived myself I had seen everything in an incredulous fog, and I had been unable to make out details; one could hardly believe what one saw. By now I had learned to interpret everything. I recognized certain S.S. chiefs. I indentified the infamous Kramer, whom the newspapers were to call "the beast of Belsen," and whose powerful silhouette dominated the scene. His cold mask, under his bristling hair, surveyed the deportees with a hard, piercing expression. Gazing at him I was fascinated, as one looking at a cobra. Never shall I forget the thin smile of satisfaction that curved on his lips at the sight of this mass of humanity so completely reduced to dependence upon his mercy.

While the deportees were being disembarked the camp orchestra, composed of inmates in striped pajamas, played swing tunes to welcome the new arrivals. The gas chamber waited, but the victims must be soothed first. Indeed, the selections at the station were usually made to the tune of languorous tangos, jazz numbers, and popular ballads.

To one side the ambulance trucks waited for the sick and aged. I have already described the first selection. The old, the sick and children under twelve or fourteen were sent to the left, the rest to the right. To the left meant the gas chamber and the crematory of Birkenau, to the right meant temporary reprieve in Auschwitz.

Everything had to be "correct" at this lugubrious ceremony. Even the S.S. troops scrupulously observed the rules of the game. They had an interest in avoiding incidents. By such tactics, a few guards could maintain order among these thousands of condemned.

Distressing episodes resulted from the separations, but the Nazis showed that they were not petty. When a young woman insisted that she would not be separated from her old mother, they often gave in and let the deportee rejoin the person she did not want to leave. Together they went to the left — to quick death.

Then, always to the sound of music — I could not help but think of the Pied Piper of the legend — the two corteges began their procession. In the meantime, the service internees had assembled the baggage. The deportees still believed they would get their possessions when they arrived at their destinations.

Other internees placed the sick into the Red Cross ambulances. They handled them tenderly until the marching columns were out of sight, then the behavior of these S.S. slaves changed so completely. Brutally, they threw the sick into the dumping trucks, as if they were sacks of potatoes, for the ambulances were now filled. As soon as everybody was pushed in, with the prisoners groaning and shouting out of sheer terror, the cargo was sent off to the crematory ovens.

Thanks to the direct evidence which I gathered through Dr. Pasche and others in the underground, I can reconstruct the last living hours of those who were sent to the left!

To the captivating tunes played by the internee musicians, whose own eyes misted with tears, the cortege of the condemned wound toward Birkenau. Fortunately, they were unconscious of the fate that awaited them. They saw a group of red brick buildings agreeably laid out and assumed it was a hospital. The S.S. troops escorting them were irreproachably "correct." They were hardly that polite dealing with selectionees from the camp, whom it was not necessary to treat with kid gloves; but the newly arrived had to be handled properly to the very end.

The condemned were led into a long underground viaduct called "Local B," which resembled the hall of a bath establishment. Up to two thousand persons could be accommodated. The "Bath Director," in a white blouse, distributed towels and soap — one more detail in the immense show. The prisoners then removed their clothing and disposed of their valuables on a huge table. Under the clothes hangers were plaques declaring in every European language, "If you want your effects when you go out, please make note of the number of your hanger."

The "bath" for which the condemned were being prepared

72

was nothing but the gas chamber, which was right off the hall. This room was equipped with many showers, the sight of which had a reassuring effect upon the deportees. But the apparatus did not function, and no water came to the faucets.

Once the condemned had filled the low, narrow gas chamber, the Germans ceased to play. The mask was down. Precautions were no longer necessary. The victims could not escape nor offer the least resistance. Sometimes the condemned, as though warned by some sixth sense, recoiled at the threshold. The Germans pushed them in brutally, not hesitating to fire their pistols into the mass. As many as possible were crowded into the room. When one or two children were left out, they were thrown on top of the heads of the adults. Then the heavy door shut like the slab of a crypt.

Horrible scenes took place within the gas chamber, although it is doubtful if the poor souls suspected even then. The Germans did not turn on the gas immediately. They waited. For the gas experts had found it was necessary to let the temperature of the room mount by a few degrees. The animal heat given off by the human herd would facilitate the action of the gas.

As the heat increased, the air fouled. Many of the condemned were said to have died before the gas was turned on.

On the ceiling of the chamber was a square opening, latticed and covered with glass. When the time came, an S.S. guard, in a gas mask, opened the peephole and released a cylinder of "Cyclone-B," a gas with a base of hydrate of cyanide which was made at Dessau.

Cyclone-B was said to have a devastating effect. Yet this did not always happen, probably because there were so many men and women to kill that the Germans economized. Besides, some of the condemned may have had high resistances. In any case, there were frequently survivors; but the Germans had no mercy. Still breathing, the dying victims were taken to the crematory and shoved into the ovens.

73

According to the evidence of former internees at Birkenau, many eminent Nazi personalities, political men and others, were present when the crematory and the gas chambers were inaugurated. They were reported to have expressed their admiration for the functional capacity of the enormous extermination plant. On the inauguration day twelve thousand Polish Jews were put to death, a minor sacrifice to the Nazi Moloch.

*   *   *   *

The Germans did let a few thousand deportees at a time live, but only to facilitate the extermination of millions of others. They made these victims perform their "dirty work." They were part of the "Sonderkommando." Three or four hundred serviced each crematory oven. Their duties consisted of pushing the condemned into the gas chambers and, after the mass murder was accomplished, of opening the doors and hauling out the corpses. Doctors and dentists were preferred for certain tasks, the latter to salvage the precious metal in the false teeth of the cadavers. The members of the Sonderkommando also had to cut the hair of the victims, a reclamation that provided additional revenue for the National Socialist economy.

Dr. Pasche, who was himself impressed into the Sonderkommando, provided me with the daily routine of the crematory personnel. For, paradoxical as it may seem — and this was not the only paradox in the camps — the Germans furnished a special doctor to care for the slaves in the extermination plant. Dr. Pasche was active in the resistance movement and at the risk of his life kept day-by-day statistics. He communicated his data only to a few of whom he was absolutely certain, in the hope that one day these figures would be brought before the world. Dr. Pasche had no illusions about what awaited him. Indeed, he was "liquidated" long before the liberation of Auschwitz.

From the eyewitness reports, one can gather what the spec-

74

tacle in the gas chamber was after the doors were opened. In their hideous suffering, the condemned had tried to crawl on top of one another. During their agonies some had dug their fingernails into the flesh of their neighbors. As a rule the corpses were so compressed and entangled that it was impossible to separate them. The German technicians invented special hook-tipped poles which were thrust deep into the flesh of the corpses to pull them out.

Once extracted from the gas chamber, the cadavers were transported to the crematory. I have already mentioned that it was not unusual that a few victims should still be alive. But they were treated as dead and were burned with the dead.

A hoist lifted the bodies into the ovens. The corpses were sorted methodically. The babies went in first, as kindling, then came the bodies of the emaciated, and finally the larger bodies.

Meanwhile the reclamation service functioned relentlessly. The dentists pulled gold and silver teeth, bridges, crowns, and plates. Other officials of the Sonderkommando gathered rings, for, despite every control some internees had kept theirs. Naturally, the Germans did not want to lose anything valuable.

The Nordic Supermen knew how to profit from everything. Immense casks were used to gather the human grease which had melted down at high temperatures. It was not surprising that the camp soap had such a peculiar odor. Nor was it astonishing that the internees became suspicious at the sight of certain pieces of fat sausage!

Even the ashes of the corpses were utilized — as fertilizer on the farms and gardens in the surrounding areas. The "surplus" was carted to the Vistula. The waters of this river carried off the remains of thousands of unfortunate deportees.

The work of the Sonderkommando was indeed the hardest and most loathsome. Two shifts worked twelve hours in relays. This staff had special quarters in the camp and contact with the other inmates was strictly forbidden. Sometimes, as punishment, they were not even permitted to go back to the camp but had to live in the building which housed the crematories. There they had enough heat, but what a ghastly place in which to eat and sleep!

The life of the members of the Sonderkommando was truly infernal. Many among them went insane. Often a husband was forced to burn his wife; a father, his children; a son, his parents; a brother, his sister.

At the end of three or four months in such an inferno the workers of the Sonderkommando were ready for their turn. The Germans had included that in the schedule. The men were gassed and then burned by those who had been brought up to take their places. The extermination plant could not let up in production even while it changed personnel.

*   *   *   *

I had then two reasons to live: one, to work with the resistance movement and help as long as I could stand upon my feet; two, to dream and pray for the day to come when I could go free and tell the world, "This is what I saw with my own eyes. It must never be allowed to happen again!"

CHAPTER XI

"Canada"

At Auschwitz-Birkenau we had a building which for some reason was called "Canada." Within its walls were stored the clothing and the other possessions taken from the deportees when they arrived at the station, or at the showers, or in the hall outside the crematory oven.

"Canada" contained vast wealth, for the Germans had encouraged the deportees to bring their valuables with them. Had they not announced in many occupied cities that it was "not against the rules" to take personal objects along? This indirect invitation proved much more effective than if they had suggested that their victims bring their jewelry. Indeed, many deportees took as much as they could in the hope of winning certain favors in return for their valuables.

A bit of everything could be found in their luggage: tobacco, fur jackets, smoked ham, even sewing machines. What a magnificent harvest for the reclamation service of the camp!

In "Canada" were specialists who did nothing but unstitch linings and soles to seek hidden treasures. The procedure must have brought results, for the Germans became generous with manpower and put nearly twelve hundred men and two thousand women into the work. Every week, one or more trains filled to bursting with products of the reclamation service left Auschwitz for Germany.

To the many objects taken from the deportees or their baggage was added the hair of the victims, from the clippings and from the corpses. Among the items in "Canada" that impressed me painfully was the row of baby carriages, which brought to mind all the unfortunate infants the Germans had executed. The children's shoes and toy section, always well stocked, was another heartrending place.

To belong to the personnel of "Canada" or to be associated with its kommandos was a great privilege for the internees. These "officials" had many opportunities to steal, and, despite the threats of severe punishment, they took advantage of them. But no such rules applied to the German officers, who often went on a tour of inspection of "Canada" and carried away a few diamonds as souvenirs in a camera or cigarette case.

Many of the kommandos stole in hopes of buying their liberty. Thanks to such bribes, many attempts to escape occurred during my stay at the camp. Generally they failed. The Germans eagerly accepted what was offered, but instead of facilitating flight, they found it more agreeable to shoot their clients.

The objects stolen from "Canada" found their way to the black market.

*　　　　*　　　　*　　　　*

Despite ferocious disciplinary measures, we had a thriving black market. Prices were determined by the scarcity of commodities, the inadequacy of rations, and, of course, by the risks involved in securing the article.

It should, therefore, not be astonishing that a pound of margarine was worth 250 gold marks, or about 100 dollars; one kilo of butter, 500 marks; one kilo of meat, 1000 marks. A cigarette cost 7 marks, but the price of a puff, or a "drag," was subject to fluctuations.

Of course, only a few could afford luxuries. Only the petty officials or the workers in "Canada" ever had the means. They had to make contact with those who worked outside the camp or with the guards themselves to exchange their valuables for money or rare commodities. In these double exchanges, they lost much. Sometimes a precious jewel would be traded for a bottle of ordinary wine.

The kitchen personnel also contributed to the traffic. They, too, were privileged, compared to the common rank of internees. They ate better in the kitchens. Besides, all those who worked there could get better clothing, thanks to the barter system. The stolen food they traded for old shoes or coats. Every evening, between five and seven o'clock, a humming black market functioned outside one of the barracks.

The barter was a natural result of local conditions. It was difficult not to take part in it. I paid eight days' ration of bread for a piece of cloth to make a nurse's blouse. I also had to pay three soups to have it sewn. Whether to feed or clothe oneself was the eternal problem facing us.

*   *   *   *

The black market brings me to the subject of the "Czech Camp" which was, for many months, an abundant source of clothing. After brief negotiations, the internees in our camp threw their rations of margarine or bread over the barbed wire to the Czech camp. In return, the Czechs tossed over articles of clothing. This was a risky business. If a guard happened by, one might be shot at. Or the clothing received in exchange might get caught on the barbed wire. But, "Nothing ventured, nothing gained," as the proverb says.

How was it that the Czechs were richer in clothing than we were? Either because of a whim of the administration, or perhaps, as was rumored, because of the energetic intervention of influential people in Czechoslovakia. Early in the summer of 1943 one of the Czech transports had been spared all the formalities; no selections, no confiscation of baggage, no hair clipping. Besides, the men were exempted from forced labor and

79

families were left together, an unheard-of favor at Birkenau. Something like a school was established for their children.

These Czechs were the only ones who, at least for a time, regularly received packages from their homes. They took advantage of official permission to ask for all sorts of useful objects, notably knitting wool with which they made warm clothing, either for their own use or for barter.

But these privileges were to last but a short time. After six months the favored treatment ended. One day, the Czechs learned that the Germans were preparing to liquidate them. They immediately decided to rebel. However, the conspiracy was a failure. At the last minute the leader, a professor from Prague, was poisoned. The Lageraelteste, a hardened criminal and a brute, got the situation in hand. The next evening more post cards were distributed to the Czechs to inform their close relatives that they were well and to ask for additional parcels. A few hours later, old and young, sick and healthy, were all exterminated.

No time was lost in bringing other Czechs to fill that camp.

I had a chance to communicate with the second train load. These Czechs, too, received favorable treatment, except for the food, which was abominable. Like little starved animals, their children wandered about the fence hoping that someone would throw over some refuse or a piece of bread.

One fine day the word went out that the second group of Czechs were being liquidated. The men were taken first, then the young women. Those who remained, the children and the aged, had no illusions. They traded everything they had for a little bread and margarine. At least they could eat their fill before dying.

That afternoon a Czech boy, who was in love with a young Vertreterin from our camp, said good-bye to her through the barbed wire that separated us. He knew how the day would end for him.

"When you see the first flames from the crematory at daybreak," he said, "you will know that it is my greeting to you."

The girl fainted. He gazed at her through the barbed wire with tears in his eyes. We helped her to get up.

"Dear," he continued, "I have a diamond that I wanted to give you as a present. I stole it while I was working in 'Canada.' But now I shall try to exchange it for a chance to go over to your camp to be with you before I die."

It was somehow arranged, and the boy came over. Everyone knew that the end of the Czech camp was near. Perhaps another day, perhaps only a few hours. The blocova left the young people alone in her room. The other inmates stood outside to watch for the Germans.

In the course of the afternoon roll call the Czechs were forced to give up their shoes. That was the unmistakable sign.

Late that night several dump trucks arrived at the camp. All who were still left in the Czech camp had to climb in. Some tried to resist; but the guards beat them or ran their hooked poles through them. Flattened against the walls of our infirmary, we witnessed this horrible scene. The little Vertreterin watched her Czech lover being pushed into the truck. Dawn found us still trembling before the wall; the last trucks had just left. Our eyes followed the smoke belching from the crematories — the remains of our poor neighbors.

During that night the young Vertreterin's hair turned almost completely white.

The first rays of the sun revealed, scattered on the ground of the Czech camp, a few abandoned items: a crust of bread, a rag doll, and some pieces of clothing. That was all that was left of the short-lived Czech village of eight thousand souls.

CHAPTER XII

The Morgue

Although I worked at the infirmary, for a while I also had to help to carry the corpses from the hospital. As though that were not enough, we had to clean the bodies, a horrible task because they had been our former patients; and besides, our supply of water for washing the living, to say nothing of the dead, was severely limited. When we were done we had to throw the dead upon a heap of rotting cadavers. When we finished we had nothing with which to disinfect or wash our own hands.

Two of us did this work. We laid the bodies on stretchers and, under the surveillance of the Germans, carried them to the morgue, a half-hour's walk from the hospital. It would have been a laborious task for healthy men. For us it was fatiguing. The guards would not let us take a breathing spell. But inhumanity was the natural order of things at Birkenau.

At the entrance to the morgue we set down the stretcher and dragged the corpses inside. We simply added them to the pile of dead. We perspired heavily but dared not wipe our faces with our contaminated hands.

Of all the horrible tasks I had to do, this one left me with the ghastliest memories. I refuse to elaborate further to describe how we had to trample over the accumulations of rotting, putrid cadavers, many of whom had died from frightful diseases. I still wonder where I got the strength necessary to keep going after such experiences. I did not even faint as did so many of my companions.

For a long time, a girl who had been a student in Warsaw helped me carry the corpses. We were beaten very often, for the Germans accused us of not being fast enough and of making a "funeral march" of this job. They cried, "Hurry up with those *Scheiss-Stucke*!" as they called the corpses, and struck us viciously.

The Polish girl was dominated by one thought — love for her mother. It was her chief topic of conversation. When she spoke of her she confided, "She is hidden in the mountains. The Germans will never find her."

But one day as we entered the morgue, she broke into hysterical laughter. I had to take her out before the Germans seized her.

Among the corpses she had just discovered the body of her beloved mother, whom she had thought so safe.

From the bodies in the morgue we could determine what physical deformations the camp life caused in the internees. After even a short stay, many of the prisoners looked like skeletons. They had lost from 50 to 60 per cent of their original weight and had shrunken in height. It was unbelievable, but they actually weighed about sixty or seventy pounds. The same cause, malnutrition, caused other bodies to become abnormally swollen.

The truth is that in the women obesity was often provoked by menstrual difficulties. After the liberation of Auschwitz, a Moscow professor, who had made many observations during the autopsies in the investigations, concluded that nine out of every ten internees revealed a distinct withering of the ovaries. Dysmenorrhea was almost a general phenomenon here.

This is no place for a scientific explanation, but it is necessary to add that a contributing factor was the constant anguish under which we lived.

The mysterious chemical powder with which the Germans dosed our food was probably one cause for the stoppage of menstruation. I personally could not obtain the proof I wanted that the Germans diluted the food with chemicals intended to dull our sexual reactions. Be that as it may, the Lageraelteste, the blocovas, and the Stubendiensts, as well as the kitchen employees, none of whom ate the ordinary camp food, were, in most cases, free from menstrual disturbances.

Indeed, I have good reason to believe that the Germans poisoned us with their mysterious powder. Once I discussed it with an inmate who worked in the kitchen. She confirmed that the order was to mix this substance into all the food given to us.

"For heaven's sake, get me a little of the powder," I pleaded. "If I ever get out of here, it will be another bit of evidence against them."

"I can't get any," she replied. "The S.S. woman mixes it into the food herself. Nobody else is allowed to go near it."

It was appalling to see how the whole physical bearing of the internees changed during their first weeks in the camp. They lost vitality and their movements became slow and apathetic; they walked with their heels turned inward. In winter their adducent muscles contracted from the cold, accentuating their abnormal carriage.

In many instances the inmates revealed signs of mental deterioration. They lost their memory and ability to concentrate. They would spend long hours staring ahead of them without the slightest sign of life. Finally they became disinterested in their fate, and, almost with complete indifference, allowed themselves to be taken to the gas chamber. This sottishness, of course, made things easier for the Germans.

*   *   *   *

I could never decide whether it was harder to dig ditches next to the crematory or work near the railroad station, where we had to collect the litter from each new convoy.

We put the scraps into large bags. There were newspapers

84

from every country, empty sardine cans, broken bottles, toys, spoons. Sometimes we had to carry the luggage from the station to "Canada," where it was piled into mountainous heaps. My duty was to bring the bags to the inmates, who sorted them by classifications: shirts into the shirt pile, toys into the toy pile, refuse into the garbage pile.

Sometimes we had to open a poor, dirty, paper box tied with a string. Occasionally, we came across expensive leather valises. At Birkenau the wealth and the poverty of all Europe met.

In the paper boxes there might be a few stale cookies wrapped in a newspaper. Some deportees had taken ground meat with them; the putrid smell filled the room. But even the hard cookies and the filthy hamburger were appetizing to us.

When we dug next to the crematory, we could hear the last cries of those who were being driven into the gas chamber. When we worked near the railroad station, it was torture to listen to the naive ones who had just arrived. Relief shone in their faces as they got off the train. Their expressions seemed to say, "We suffered on the trip, but now, thank God, we are here." The sight of them helping each other down, arranging a scarf, buttoning a child's coat, recalled my own arrival at the camp and my subsequent disillusionment.

How could I prevent them from making the same mistakes I had made? They were already passing before the official table for the first selection. I tried to edge toward the women as they passed to whisper to them:

"Tell them that your son is over twelve . . . . Don't let your daughter say that she is ill . . . . Tell your son to stand up very straight . . . . Always tell them that you are in good health." The line continued to move before his table.

The women looked at me in surprise. They asked "Why?" and looked at me as though to say, "What does this dirty woman want? She must be mad."

No, they could not understand the importance of what I was saying. There was scorn in their eyes. What could women in dirty rags tell them? It could not occur to them that they, too, might become ragged creatures. And so the same tragedies were repeated. Seeking to spare their children from hard labor, they lied about their ages and unwittingly sent them to the gas chamber.

In the midst of the chaos, the Germans shouting, the prisoners babbling, they were separated into two groups: right and left! — life and death!

*   *   *   *

I was still watching the transports when, to my amazement, four men in sport clothes left the ranks. They were fair-haired and sleek, although their grooming was ruffled from the long journey. The guards sought to push them back, but they insisted on speaking to the "commander."

One of the German officers who was standing about observed what was going on and signaled to the soldiers to let the men approach. I was about ten yards away but I heard their loud conversation. I was surprised to hear that they were speaking in English!

The German officer obviously understood them, but after the first exchange he insisted that they speak German. One man managed a sort of broken German and interpreted for the group. They referred to another camp from which they had been transferred, and insisted that the Germans had no right to move them.

The German officer was obviously amused. "We have no right?" he asked with a sarcastic smile.

"Of course you haven't," replied the sportily dressed interpreter, "we are not Jews!"

"We are not interested whether you are Jews or not. You are Americans!" came the retort.

"I demand that you treat us according to International Law."

"Of course," the German officer returned smoothly. "We

shall forward your request directly to the American Government. If you will be patient, we may be able to deliver the message in Washington personally."

"Take the gentlemen to the American Camp," another officer commanded.

The soldiers adjusted their rifles and "heiled" the officer. They marched the little group off toward the forest, 150 feet away. A few minutes later I heard several gunshots. But shooting was so common at Birkenau that I paid no attention.

Meanwhile, the music played and the columns of deportees dragged on.

A few weeks later, I was sorting the luggage "reclaimed" from the railroad station. I found a group of suitcases that looked alike. They all contained shirts with American labels, tennis racquets, sweaters, cameras, and photographs of couples with children.

We even found several phonograph records in one suitcase. An old inmate, hungry for music, hurriedly put one on a little portable phonograph which we had found in the luggage. A beautiful, clear voice sang a Christmas carol. We were touched. The other prisoners halted at their tasks and listened.

A German guard, evidently hearing the music, rushed into the room. He kicked the phonograph with his boot and smashed the record. When we had gathered the pieces, I read the label. We had been listening to "Silent Night," sung by Bing Crosby. For a few moments the American crooner had helped us to forget our lot in Auschwitz.

I began to throw the photographs on the garbage heap, as the rules required. Suddenly, a picture caught my attention. "I've seen those faces somewhere," I thought.

Then I remembered. These were the Americans I had seen at the station.

"Where is the American camp?" I asked the old inmate.

"You stupid thing," she said crossly, "don't you know there is no American camp?"

87

"But I heard that there was one," I insisted.

"All right, if that is the way you want it. The American camp is in the same place as the old folks' and the children's camp.

"You mean they dared to kill the Americans?" I asked. "Is it possible?"

She smirked, "Americans are so much more fuel for the crematory ovens. In the eyes of the Germans they are only enemies, like us. Killing was never a problem for the Germans. They take them to the woods and shoot them. That is the American camp."

CHAPTER XIII

The "Angel of Death" vs. the "Grand Selector"

I was to have died that day. Not even when I was "selected" had I been so close to death. When I think of it I see myself dead, and fancy that I am returning from another world.

Had Irma Griese been less curious, I should have perished. But she was apparently too intent on finding out why Dr. Fritz Klein, the S.S. physician in charge of the women's camp at Auschwitz and later at Bergen-Belsen, had created a post expressly for me, tatter of humanity that I was, close-cropped, dirty, dressed in filthy rags, a man's unmated old shoes on my feet. Because she wanted to know, I was saved.

At that time the "selections" were made by the chief camp directresses, Hasse and Irma Griese. On Mondays, Wednesdays, and Saturdays, the roll calls lasted from dawn until the end of the afternoon, when they had their full quota of victims.

When these two women appeared at the camp entrance, the internees, who already knew what to expect, became panic-stricken.

The beautiful Irma Griese advanced toward the prisoners with a swinging gait, her hips in play, and the eyes of forty thousand wretched women, mute and motionless, upon her. She was of medium height, elegantly attired, with her hair faultlessly dressed. The mortal terror which her mere presence inspired visibly pleased her. For this twenty-two-year-old girl was completely without pity. With a sure hand she chose her vic-

89

tims, not only from the well but from the sick, the feeble, and the incapacitated. Those who, despite hunger and torture, still evidenced a glimmer of their former physical beauty were the first to be taken. They were Irma Griese's special targets.

During the "selections," the "blonde angel of Belsen," as she was later to be called by the press, made liberal use of her whip. She slashed wherever she wished, and we endured as well as we could. Our shrieks of pain and our spurts of blood made her smile. What faultless, pearly teeth she had!

One day in June, 1944, 315 "selected" women were pushed together into a washroom. In the big hall the unfortunate ones had already been kicked and whipped. Then Irma Griese commanded the S.S. guards to nail the door shut. As simple as that.

Before being sent to the gas chamber they would have to pass in review before Dr. Klein. But he made them wait three days. During this time the condemned women lay crushed together on the concrete floor without food or drink or the use of a latrine. They were human beings, but who cared about that?

My companions knew that I accompanied Dr. Klein on his rounds. They begged me to lead him toward the washroom to rescue some poor souls in there. Some pleaded with me to intercede for the life of a friend, a mother, or a sister.

On the day Dr. Klein was to arrive, I felt my heart beating in my throat. I must snatch at least a few of these creatures from death, no matter what the cost.

"Herr Oberarzt," I said to him, trembling all over, as we began our rounds, "surely there must have been some mistake in the last selections. There are people shut up in the washroom who are not sick. Perhaps it's not worth while to send them to the hospital." I pretended that I did not know of the existence of the gas chamber.

"But you don't even have medicaments," remarked Dr. Klein. "Besides, your directress selected them herself. I can't do much about it."

90

This was before our camp had either a hospital or an infirmary, and I dared not propose that we take care of the sick ourselves. We had internee doctors for each barrack, but they had no medicines!

I decided to try to cajole Dr. Klein. "These poor women have no one any more," I said. "They have no home, no family. But some still have a mother, a sister, or a child in the camp. I implore you, doctor, don't separate them. Think of your own sister and mother if you have one!"

Dr. Klein did not reply. I had been talking as we headed for the washroom. Now we were there. A brief word of command and the S.S. guards forced the nailed door. We entered.

There were the 315 who had been shut up for three days and nights. Many had already died. Others, no longer able to stand, were squatting on the corpses. Still others, veritable skeletons, were already too feeble to get up. Shut in the darkness for three days, they were blinking now, with their hands before their faces.

They shouted, "We haven't had anything to eat in three days. We are not sick! I don't want to go to the hospital!"

Dr. Klein, who was usually calm, the only German in Auschwitz who never shouted, lost his head. His face crimson, he suddenly yelled: "What's going on at that barrack? Don't they want to work any more? Do they intend to send everybody to us at the hospital? I'll teach them, I will! Get out! You're nothing but a pack of malingerers!"

I shuddered before this burst of rage. Then, as I saw him driving several of the stronger people toward the exit, I understood. "Look, Doctor, there's another fake invalid!" I said. I pointed to a young girl, a gifted mathematician.

"Get out! Don't let me see you again," shouted Dr. Klein.

Later, the sinister death trucks appeared and carried off 284 other victims to the gas chambers. Thirty-one we saved that day from certain death. All because Dr. Klein was aroused to a rare gesture of humanity — for an S.S.

91

The following Sunday we were punished. I don't remember why. But it was not the first time we had spent Sunday in front of the barracks on our knees, in the mud, for it had rained that morning.

We had been kneeling for an eternity. Time seemed to have stopped. Rain began to fall again. We had to remain on our knees, motionless, with our arms lifted to the sky. A sliver of glass had cut my right knee, but I dared not stir for fear of additional punishment.

Suddenly, I was called. Dr. Klein had summoned me. I got up and ran to the camp gate where he was waiting. "I have never come to the camp on Sunday," he declared, "but as I promised yesterday to bring you medicaments for your invalids I have made an exception. Here, I have brought you a number of samples of medicine."

As I held out my arm to accept the large carton I felt a hand on my shoulder. I turned. It was Irma Griese, armed with her whip!

"What are you doing there, you pig!" she shrieked. "Don't you know that you may not leave the ranks?"

"I had her summoned," answered Dr. Klein for me.

"You have no right to do that, Herr Oberarzt. This is Sunday, and you have no business to be here."

"You have the audacity to forbid my coming?"

"And why not?" sneered Griese. "I have a perfect right to do so. Do not forget, Doctor, that I give the orders here."

"Maybe so, but not to me," he retorted. "As head physician, I have the right to come when I think fit."

The beautiful Irma Griese bit her lips, but she was undefeated. She vented her spleen on me. "To your place, at once, you filthy scum!" she fumed.

"No, not right away," Klein put in, calmly.

"You have nothing to say about it, Herr Oberarzt. For a long time your conduct has been most strange. You set free some of the patients shut up in the washroom. You come to the camp on Sundays, ostensibly to bring medicines, but actually to meddle in affairs that do not concern you. You have contravened my orders, and you will have to answer for it."

"I take the responsibility for everything. I am an S.S. major-physician."

"I warn you, Oberarzt, that you are playing a dangerous game."

"That is my affair. Don't you worry about me. Come," he added, "follow me." He beckoned to me as though Irma Griese no longer existed.

We started off along the Lagerstrasse between the two rows of barracks. The blonde "Angel of death" stood there, rooted to the ground and shaking with rage.

Everyone in the camp knew how vindictive Irma Griese could be. My situation was fraught with peril. I tried to hide, but it was no use. Where could a person hide in Auschwitz?

Two hours after Dr. Klein had left me I was standing on the large wolfskin that served as a rug in Griese's office. I knew what she had in store for me. Someone had to pay for her humiliation. I would be the one. Very well, if they would kill me at once, without hideous tortures. I knew what the merciless torturers could do.

"Who are you? Where did you make Dr. Klein's acquaintance? In what language do the two of you speak?" Irma Griese asked me in a single breath, her periwinkle eyes gleaming with hatred.

"The Oberarzt comes from the same region as I, from Transylvania, and I speak to him in my native tongue. I first came to know him here in the camp. I am a medical student," I said.

"Well, well! and your name?" asked Irma Griese.

An astonishing question at Auschwitz-Birkenau, where we were only numbers, and not women.

Meanwhile, the blonde devil had risen from her seat. "Henceforth I forbid you to accompany Dr. Klein on his rounds. If he addresses you, you will not answer. If he sends for you,

you will not come. Understand? And now, answer me. Why did you disobey me? Why didn't you return to roll call as soon as I ordered you?"

"I am a member of the Infirmary Staff. I thought I ought to obey Dr. Klein."

"Oh, that's what you thought. I'm the one you must obey, I alone!"

With calculated deliberation, she took her revolver from her desk and advanced toward me. We were a striking contrast, I, close-cropped, clad in rags, dirty, drenched from the rain, and she with her cleverly done hair, her striking beauty, and her artful make-up. Her impeccably tailored suit showed off her lovely figure.

"You swine," she hissed between her teeth. I cringed from the cold barrel of her revolver as she passed it over my left temple. I felt her hot breath. "You're afraid, aren't you?"

Suddenly, the butt of her gun came down on my head, once, twice, again and again. She struck me full in the face with her fist, again and again.

I tasted my blood. I stumbled. I toppled on the wolfskin.

When I opened my eyes I was lying outside in the mud, exposed to the rain which was still falling. The camp bell was ringing for another "selection." Bruised, covered with blood, I picked myself up and ran toward my barrack in order not to miss the roll call.

As I turned, I saw Irma Griese coming from the Fuehrer-stube, her whip in hand, to designate the next batch for the gas chamber. Why she did not send me there, or shoot me, or put me to death in some more evil fashion, I could never guess.

CHAPTER XIV

"Organization"

"We have to hold on," an old internee, who was working on the road in our camp, had whispered the day we arrived. Our hair was freshly clipped, and we shivered in our rags, waiting for the ambulances to let us pass. "To be able to hold on," he added, "there is one thing to do: organize."

During the long days that followed I often wondered what the man had meant by this word, "organize." Organize what? It took me longer to comprehend the real meaning of "organize." I put two and two together. The old stone-breaker's counsel, plus the exhortations of other internees, gave me my answer. "If you do not want to die of hunger, there is only one thing to do: steal." Suddenly I understood: to "organize" meant to steal.

Events confirmed my interpretation. Yet the term "organize" contained a nuance that I did not grasp for some time. It meant not only to steal, but to steal at the expense of the Germans. In this way, theft became ennobled, and even beneficial to the internees. When the employees of "Canada" or of the "Beklei-dungskammer" stole warm clothing for their badly clothed comrades, that was not common theft; it was an act of social solidarity. The more one took from the Germans and sent into the barracks of the camp for the use of the internees instead of letting it be dispatched into Germany, the more one helped the cause.

Thus, the words, "steal" and "organize" were not at all synonymous.

Unfortunately, it was not always easy to draw the line. Man frequently speaks loftily of his less noble deeds. And the term "organization" was often used to excuse low theft.

"You have taken my bread ration," an internee would cry, "This is thievery!"

"Oh, I'm sorry," the accused one would reply, "I didn't know it was yours. And don't accuse me of stealing . . . . It was 'organization.'"

Alas, under that pretext, some inmates pressed by hunger stole the miserable rations of their neighbors. Many who were inadequately clothed snatched the poor rags of others in the washroom.

Yet in the melting pot of Auschwitz-Birkenau, social barriers fell away and class prejudice vanished. Simple, uncultured peasant women accomplished wonders in the way of "organization," and gave proof of magnificent selflessness, while sophisticated women whose morality had never been doubted pretended to engage in "organization" to the detriment of their comrades. Their acts may not have had serious consequences, but they were nonetheless significant.

In September, 1944, our friend L. succeeded in "organizing" five spoons. He generously gave them to members of the infirmary staff who had taken care of him. I did not know how to express my joy when I received this simple object, a common thing in civilized life. For months I had eaten without using either spoon or fork, reduced, like the others, to lapping my food out of the bowl like a dog. So the spoon made me very happy.

Imagine then my disappointment when, a few days later, it disappeared. I made a thorough investigation and uncovered the truth: the thief was none other than the wife of one of the richest industrialists of Hungary, a multimillionaress, and accustomed to truly fabulous luxuries. At Birkenau, where only human beings endowed with exceptional moral stamina could remain honest and good, the ex-millionairess had proven that she was not sufficiently endowed.

This incident alarmed me for the future of these internees if they ever left the camps alive. For the present, however, we had all we could do to live through each day.

*   *   *   *

I had been at the infirmary several weeks when a friend told me that an internee in Barrack No. 9 named Malika was selling woolen material in exchange for bread and margarine. I desperately needed a warm jacket. I had no bread or margarine, but I had a friend from whom I could borrow some.

Malika was a policewoman whose function was to use her stick to chase the inmates from the barbed wire fence. Many deportees sought to communicate with the Czech camp. It was Malika's duty to prevent barter transactions.

She carried out her duties conscientiously. During her hours of duty no one could negotiate with the Czechs. That is, no one except Malika herself. She had a complete monopoly. And the former fruit vendor became one of the leading "business women" in the camp.

The friend who gave me the information intended to buy herself a white blouse, so she accompanied me to Barrack No. 9. Malika was not there. We waited.

We had set aside the day's ration for the purchase of the clothing, and we were both tortured by hunger. From the barrack, tantalizing aromas drifted to us. The "Califactorka," the blocova's servant, was preparing a plate of "plazki" for her mistress. To internees like us plazki was an unattainable dream. It was a kind of pancake made of grated potatoes and bread crumbs, and fried in margarine. Only the blocovas and a few other officials could afford such a delicacy, and even they only occasionally. We could not help but glance enviously at the frying pan. How we sighed over the tempting fragrance!

The Califactorka signaled to us. "I will make a deal with you," she said in a low tone. "Bring me a few aspirin tablets and I will give you a bit of plazki. I have a bad pain in my ear, and I don't want to wait in line outside the infirmary."

My friend drew me to one side. I appreciated the battle that was going on inside her. She had two aspirin tablets with her. Now aspirin was very scarce in camp, and each tablet represented a treasure. Did we have the right to barter them for personal profit? We wrestled with our consciences, while the aroma of the plazki tormented our nostrils.

My friend finally made the decision. "Since the Califactorka has a pain, she would get the aspirin at the infirmary anyway. All we do is save her the time of standing in line. It could be no crime to give it to her now? You agree?"

Weakly, I agreed. Yet, in our hearts, we knew that we had no right to do this. For the infirmary supplies were so limited that we had to reserve our aspirin for graver cases than earaches. Even had she stood in line, it is doubtful that the Califactorka would have received any. Whether she would or would not have received any is immaterial. We had abused our standing in the camp for our personal welfare. In normal circumstances I doubt that either my friend or I would have stooped so low. But we were at Birkenau-Auschwitz, and we were starved.

Discreetly my friend slipped the two aspirin tablets to the Califactorka. She, in return, divided a plazki in two with her dirty hands and stealthily passed it to us.

I exchanged a furtive look with my friend. We were both blushing for shame.

CHAPTER XV

Accursed Births

The most poignant problem that faced us in caring for our companions was that of the accouchements. As soon as a baby was delivered at the infirmary, mother and child were both sent to the gas chamber. That was the unrelenting decision of our masters. Only when the infant was not likely to survive or when it was stillborn was the mother ever spared and allowed to return to her barrack. The conclusion we drew from this was simple: the Germans did not want the newborn to live; if they did, the mothers, too, must die.

We five whose responsibility it was to bring these infants into the world — the world of Birkenau-Auschwitz — felt the burden of this monstrous conclusion which defied all human and moral law. That it was also nonsensical from a medical point of view, did not matter for the moment. How many sleepless nights we spent turning this tragic dilemma over in our minds. And in the morning the mothers and their babies both went to their deaths.

One day we decided we had been weak long enough. We must at least save the mothers. To carry out our plan, we would have to make the infants pass for stillborn. Even so, many precautions must be taken, for if the Germans were ever to suspect it, we, too, would be sent to the gas chambers — and probably to the torture chamber first.

Now when we were notified that a woman's labor pains had

started during the day, we did not take the patient to the infirmary. We stretched her out on a blanket in one of the bottom koias of the barrack in the presence of her neighbors.

When the pains began during the night we ventured to take the woman to the infirmary, for at least in the dark we might proceed comparatively unobserved. In the koia we could hardly make a decent examination. In the infirmary we had our examination table. Still we lacked antisepsis, and the danger of infection was enormous, for this was the same room in which we treated purulent wounds!

Unfortunately, the fate of the baby always had to be the same. After taking every precaution, we pinched and closed the little tike's nostrils and when it opened its mouth to breathe, we gave it a dose of a lethal product. An injection might have been quicker, but that would have left a trace and we dared not let the Germans suspect the truth.

We placed the dead infant in the same box which had brought it from the barrack, if the accouchement had taken place there. As far as the camp administration was concerned, this was a stillbirth.

And so, the Germans succeeded in making murderers of even us. To this day the picture of those murdered babies haunts me. Our own children had perished in the gas chambers and were cremated in the Birkenau ovens, and we dispatched the lives of others before their first voices had left their tiny lungs. Often I sit and think what kind of fate would these little creatures, snuffed out on the threshold of life, have had? Who knows? Perhaps we killed a Pasteur, a Mozart, an Einstein. Even had those infants been destined to uneventful lives, our crimes were no less terrible. The only meager consolation is that by these murders we saved the mothers. Without our intervention they would have endured worse sufferings, for they would have been thrown into the crematory ovens while still alive.

Yet I try in vain to make my conscience acquit me. I still see the infants issuing from their mothers. I can feel their warm little bodies as I held them. I marvel to what depths these Germans made us descend!

*   *   *   *

Our masters did not wait for births to take action against fertility in Auschwitz. Intermittently — for all their measures, without exception, were intermittent and subject to capricious change — they sent all pregnant women to the gas chamber.

Generally, pregnant women who came in the Jewish transports were immediately ordered to the left when they arrived at the station. The women usually wore several layers of clothing, one on top of the other, which they hoped to keep. So even obvious cases of pregnancy were difficult to discover before the deportees were made to shed their apparel. Besides, they could not count on the preliminary control to catch the very early pregnancies.

Even inside the camp it was not easy to determine which women were in the family way. For the word went around that it was extremely dangerous to be found pregnant. Those who arrived in this condition, therefore, hid themselves when they could and, to this end, had the active cooperation of their neighbors.

Incredible as it may seem, some succeeded in concealing their conditions to the last moment, and the deliveries took place secretly in the barracks. I shall never, as long as I live, forget the morning when, during roll call, in the midst of the deathlike silence among the thousands of deportees, a piercing cry rose. A woman had unexpectedly been seized with her first labor pains. It is not necessary to describe what happened to this poor soul.

It was not long before the Germans noticed that in the successive trains of deportees an extraordinarily low percentage of pregnancies was reported. They decided to take more energetic measures; one could always depend upon them for that.

101

The barrack doctors, whose duty it was to report pregnant women, received rigorous orders. Nevertheless, I more than once saw the doctors defy every danger and certify that a woman was not pregnant when they positively knew that she was. Dr. G. stood up to the infamous Dr. Mengerle, medical director of the camp, and denied every case of pregnancy that could possibly be contested. Later, the camp infirmary somehow secured a pharmaceutical product which, through injection, brought about premature births. What could we do? Wherever possible, the doctors resorted to this procedure, which was certainly the lesser horror for the mother.

Still, the number of pregnancies remained unbelievably low, and the Germans resorted to their usual trickery. They announced that pregnant women, even such Jewesses as were still alive, would be treated with special regard. They would be allowed to remain away from roll call, to receive a larger ration of bread and soup, and be permitted to sleep in a special barrack. Finally, the promise was made that they would be transferred to a hospital as soon as their time came. "The camp is not a maternity ward," proclaimed Dr. Mengerle. This tragically true statement appeared to offer great hopes to many of the unfortunate women.

Why should anyone here believe anything the Germans said? First, because many never saw the final horrors until it was too late for them to communicate the truth to their neighbors. Second, because no human being could fathom the ends of which they were capable, which they plotted daily, and which was part of their master plan for world conquest.

Dr. Mengerle never missed the chance to ask the women indiscreet and improper questions. He made no secret of his amusement when he learned that one of the pregnant deportees had not seen her soldier husband for many months. Another time he hunted out a fifteen-year-old girl whose pregnancy was clearly dated from her arrival in the camp. He questioned her at length and insisted on the most intimate details. When his

102

curiosity was finally satisfied, he sent her off with the next herd of selectionees. The camp was no maternity ward. It was only the antechamber to Hell.

CHAPTER XVI

Small Details of Living Behind Barbed Wire

Toward the end of November, 1944, the German vigilance relaxed somewhat. We especially appreciated the disappearance of the German guards who had previously marched along the barbed wire. Now, the men and women of the neighboring camps were comparatively free to exchange a few words through the fences.

The spectacle was unforgettable. The couples were separated by an electrically charged fence, the slightest contact with which was fatal. They stood knee deep in the snow in the shadow of the crematory ovens, and made "plans" for the future, and traded the latest gossip.

If only these rendezvous had been authorized and, therefore, without danger. But these meetings were still forbidden. The respite was only temporary. All that was necessary to end it was for an S.S. guard to begin firing at the group. Occasionally a sly or sadistic guard would wait half an hour or an hour on purpose, until the couples had increased in number. Then a shot fired into the crowd would not be ammunition wasted. But they paid no attention to this menace. Human nature can get used to anything, even to the continual presence of death. For a bit of pleasure they risked any danger. And pleasures were so rare, and life was so cheap at Auschwitz-Birkenau!

One Sunday afternoon a pretty young Hungarian girl, about twenty years old, was brought to the infirmary. She had been wounded by a shot in the eyes. I learned that she had made the acquaintance of a French deportee, a student who had been arrested as a member of the underground. Meeting in front of the barbed wire, they had fallen in love. On this particular day a guard had amused himself by firing into the crowd. The bullet had lodged in the girl's right eye.

Her face covered with blood, the unfortunate girl begged us to tell her if she would regain her sight. "If I can never see Georges again, what is the use of living? I don't want to be blind!"

We carried her to Camp F, where she was operated on. Her right eye had to be removed, and the left eye was also in danger. We could not tell her that. Instead, we assured her that everything would be fine again in a few months.

An hour later, another crowd had collected in front of the barbed wire. The accident had been forgotten.

The barbed wire was the very symbol of our captivity. But it also had the power to liberate. Each morning the workers found deformed bodies on the high tension wires. That was how many chose to put an end to their torments. A special detail detached the corpses with hooked sticks. The sight of the misshapen dead filled us with mixed sentiments. We were sorry for them, for such deaths were really horrible; yet we envied them, too. They had found the courage to reject a life which no longer merited the name.

*   *   *   *

In the camps of Auschwitz-Birkenau and, later, everywhere, many stories circulated about the tattooing of the prisoners. One would think that all the internees were tattooed upon arrival. Some believed the tattooing safeguarded one against being sent to the gas chamber, or that, at least, a special authorization from Berlin would be necessary before a registered-tattooed internee could be put to death. Even in our camp many were convinced of that.

Actually, as in so many matters, there was no fixed regulation. Sometimes all deportees were tattooed when they arrived. Then again there was laxity, and over a period of months the ordinary deportees were not tattooed at all.

The inmates of Birkenau were directed into their camps without matriculation numbers. Undoubtedly such formalities appeared superfluous even to the Germans, for these people were merely to be fuel for the crematory ovens.

As for the tattooings conferred upon the deportees, that was highly questionable. All who had some sort of responsibility, the blocovas and other minor officials and those who worked in the hospitals were tattooed. These were no longer "Haftling" but "Schutzhaftling" (protected prisoners). At the Schreibstube they received individual cards containing their names and other data. In case of natural death, the card had all the information. In case of execution, "S B," that is to say, "Sonderbehandlung" (special treatment), was added. Those who were not tattooed had no record of death in the files. They were no more than digits in the "production" statistics of the extermination plant.

The tattooing operation was carried out by the deportees employed at the "Politische Buro" (Political Bureau). They used a metal-tipped stylus. They inscribed the registration number on the skin of the arm, the back, or the chest. The ink which it injected under the skin was indelible.

When a tattooed person died, his registration number became "available" for the next deportee, since the Germans for some reason never went beyond the number 200,000. When they reached that point, they started over again with a new serial letter. The racial deportees had a triangle or a Star of David with their numbers.

The tattooing operation was painful and always was followed by inflammation and swelling. It is impossible to estimate the effect it had on morale. A tattooed woman felt that her life was finished; she was no longer anything but a number.

106

I was number "25,403." I still have it on my right arm and shall carry it with me to the grave.

*   *   *   *

Tattooing was not the only method employed to stigmatize the deportees. The Germans also marked us with obvious signs to indicate nationality or category. On our clothing above the heart we wore a triangular insignia on a piece of white cloth. The letter P, meant Polish; the letter R, Russian. "N. N." (*Nacht und Nebel*) indicated that the wearer was condemned to death. This term (night and fog) was borrowed from a Dutch secret organization. In the camp we had no idea what "N. N." could mean. I learned about it later from members of the underground.

There were many Polish and Russian prisoners of war, but the French Army was also represented. A few distinguished names were Lieutenant-Colonel Robert Blum, Knight of the Legion of Honor and chief of the resistance movement in the Grenoble region; Captain Rene Dreyfus, Knight of the Legion of Honor and the nephew of Alfred Dreyfus; and Physician-General Job, who was killed in spite of his seventy-six years as were the Colonel and the Captain.

Among the "nameless" in Birkenau-Auschwitz, we found inmates who, before their captivity, were called Genevieve De Gaulle and Daniel Casanova — both important members of the French resistance movement.

The color of the insignia varied with the category of the internee. The "associates," that is to say, the saboteurs, the prostitutes, and any who sought to escape work, wore a black triangle. The green triangle was reserved for common criminals. There were also rose and violet triangles, but these were rare. The first indicated homosexuals; the second adherents of the sect, "Bibelforschers." The clothing of the Jewish inmates was marked with a red stripe down the back and their triangle was trimmed with a yellow band. At Birkenau, these insignia took the place of identity cards.

Incidentally, the people in the camp were chiefly Gentile, rather than Jewish, as many western readers may assume. Indeed, the population of Auschwitz was about 80 per cent Gentile. The reason was no secret. Most of the Jews were immediately sent to the gas chambers and the crematory ovens. The events I describe happened to Catholics, Protestants, and Greek Orthodox — to all, who, like the Jews, were for one reason or another regarded by the German masters as expendables.

*   *   *   *

Birkenau contained many nuns and priests, mostly Polish. Some had been members of, or had aided, the underground. Others had been arrested on denunciation, or perhaps for no reason other than whim.

Religious practices were forbidden in the camp under pain of immediate death. The Germans regarded all churchmen as superfluous and assigned them to the most difficult tasks. Indeed, the tortures and humiliations to which the priests were subjected was frequently more horrible than any other I had ever seen. The clerics were used for various experiments, including castration.

In 1944 a large number of priests arrived in Auschwitz. They were put through the usual formalities: bathing, clipping, and search. The Germans took away their prayer books, crucifixes, and other religious objects, and gave them the striped prisoners' rags. To the surprise of the internee officials, the priests were not ordered to be tattooed. But the Germans did nothing without cunning. Even before the priests had entered the "baths," the administration had given the word that they were to be killed that evening.

At the end of September, a Protestant minister from England,

108

and L. were ordered to empty a huge ditch which was filled with water.

"You are the Allied Powers, and the water in the ditch is the German strength!" shouted the S.S. guard. "Empty the ditch!"

The two men carried pails of water for hours, panting under the lash, for the Germans watched, whipped them, and laughed. The water remained at the same level. The ditch was fed by a spring. German humor.

At the hospital, I came to know many deportee nuns. One became my close friend. Since the fall of Poland she had passed through several prisons and, in the course of interrogations, had been many times mistreated and beaten. The Germans never accused her of any specific crime or fault. Had they done so she might have been condemned to a prison term and might have had an easier life than in the camp.

At Birkenau she suffered unbelievable humiliations. When they took her nun's robe away, the German guards fell upon the notion of dressing themselves in it. To bring spice into their pleasantry, they performed obscene dances in her presence. She was forced to march before the S.S. troops in the nude. German sport.

The Germans assembled a large collection of nuns' habits and gave them to the women in their brothels.

In our camp the Sisters shared the same existence as we all did. Their hardest privations I dare say came from the restrictions on their religious lives: no mass, no confession, no sacraments.

A nun who was about thirty was brought to our hospital after she had undergone X-ray experiments. Despite the pain caused by the experiments, she bore up with great courage. She prayed silently all day and asked for nothing. When we inquired about her condition, she replied, "Thank you. There are many who have suffered much more than I."

Her patient smiles tortured us, but also inspired us. We knew how horribly she was suffering. Yet there was nothing we could do to help her.

While being searched upon her arrival, she had protested firmly when her rosary beads and holy pictures were taken from her. The Germans had beaten her, torn the holy objects from her hands, and stamped upon them.

Even then she had fearlessly declared, "No nation can exist without God."

The Germans could have killed her at once. But they knew death would be easy compared to their other methods. So they had sent her to the experimental station. From there she was brought to our hospital. After a few days, the Germans announced her transfer to another "camp."

Those were miserable hours that we spent waiting for them to come for her. We were excited, and some of us cried. But the nun lay there with a peaceful expression on her countenance.

"Do not be sorry for me," she said. "I am going to my Lord. But we must say good-bye to each other. Let us pray."

Silently, the other women, whether Protestant, Catholic, or Jew, prayed with her. Even those who had lost their faith joined us to comfort her last hours. We were still praying when the Germans arrived with their death truck.

The priests and nuns in the camp proved that they had real strength of character. One rarely met that except in deportees who were animated by faith in an ideal. Apart from the clerics, only the active members of the underground, or the militant communists, had that spirit.

Many of the ecclesiasts were executed shortly after they arrived. Frequently, those who escaped the first selection succumbed to disease. The rest were driven to death with fiendish deliberation. Indeed, the nuns and priests of the martyred countries paid a heavy toll to the Germans.

*   *   *   *

At Camp D, which was a men's enclosure, a barrack was

110

reserved for male children. One afternoon the S.S. assembled all the youngsters, called the roll, and proceeded to make a selection. How they had survived the initial selection upon arrival I do not know, unless for some reason none had been made at that time. The procedure they used was weird. A cord was stretched to a certain height. All who passed under this mark were automatically set aside for the gas chambers. Of one hundred children, only five or six survived.

By the end of the afternoon the adult internees looked on, numbly, while twenty trucks laden with these naked children, shivering from the cold, pulled away toward Birkenau. As the trucks passed, the children cried out their names so that their parents might be notified.

Most of the little condemned boys knew what their fate would be. So it was amazing that they bore up at all. Apparently, the camp had matured them, for they accepted the news with more *sang froid* than the strongest adults ever did.

One internee told me that he had been in their barrack while they waited for the trucks. The children were sitting on the floor, wide-eyed and silent. He asked one lad, "Well, how are you, Janeck?"

With a thoughtful expression on his face, the child answered, "Everything is so bad here that it can only be better 'over there.' I am not afraid."

I spoke to a twelve-year-old boy from the Czech camp who was wandering along the barbed wire, looking for something to eat. After speaking to him for a few minutes, I said, "Karli, do you know that you are too clever?"

"Yes," was the reply, "I know that I am very clever. But I know, too, that I shall never have a chance to be more clever. That is what is tragic."

The story circulated throughout the camp about how bravely one little boy behaved before he climbed the truck which was to take him to the gas chamber.

"Don't cry, Pista," he begged another Hungarian youngster,

111

"haven't you seen that our grandparents, our fathers, our mothers, and our sisters were killed? It is our turn now."

Before he entered the truck, he turned to the S.S. with a grim expression. He said to the German, "But one thing gives me pleasure. Very soon you will croak, too."

That evening as I was cleaning the latrine pit of the hospitals, I found myself aided by a group of fifteen- or sixteen-year-old boys from Camp D. These were the sole survivors of the mass liquidation. They confided that members of the Sonderkommando, though calloused by the murders they were compelled to perform, had been so indignant that, at the risk of their own lives, they had let a few victims slip through. These children had rejoined their comrades. How long they would be free before the Germans noticed it no one could say.

Once more the mothers in our camp spent a sleepless night. How could they sleep, for they were eternally haunted by the fear that their children had been liquidated at Camp D? Many still could not believe that most of the children had been exterminated as soon as they arrived.

*　　　*　　　*　　　*

Camp E was the home of the Gypsies. Most of its eight thousand occupants were Bohemians who had been transported from Germany. But there were also some from Hungary, Czechoslovakia, Poland, and even from France. For a while their living conditions were better than in the other camps. Indeed, they were clothed almost becomingly, while we were dressed like scarecrows. Their food was edible, and they enjoyed various liberties that were forbidden to the other internees. Occasionally, they abused these privileges and when they had the opportunity exploited the other deportees, to the amusement of the Germans.

Then one day all that changed. The authorities had decided. On the first of August the German head physician assembled all the internee doctors in Camp E and made them sign a paper stating that grave epidemics of typhus, scarlet fever, etc., were raging in Camp E.

One doctor courageously reminded the German that there were relatively few sick in this camp and no contagious cases.

The S.S. chief doctor replied ironically: "Since you have such a lively interest in the fate of these internees, you shall follow them into their new home." By "new home," he meant, of course, the crematory oven.

A few hours later, the trucks arrived. The departure of the Gypsies was marked by several incidents. Suspicious of what was in store, a few Gypsies tried to hide on the roof, in the wash-rooms, and in the ditches. They were rounded up one after another.

I cannot forget the cry of one Hungarian Gypsy mother. She had forgotten that death waited for all of them. She thought only of her child as she pleaded, "Don't take my little boy from me. Don't you see that he is sick?"

The shouting of the S.S. and the weeping of the children awakened the occupants of the neighboring camps. They were the horrified witnesses of the departure of the trucks. Later that night the long red flames flashed from the chimneys of the crematory building. What crime had the Gypsies committed? They were a minority, and that was enough to condemn them to death.

*　　　*　　　*　　　*

The extermination of the Jews — Polish, Lithuanian, French, etc., — was carried out in groups by national regions. The extermination of the Jews of Hungary took place in the summer of 1944. This mass liquidation was without precedent even in the annals of Birkenau. In July, 1944, the five crematory ovens, the mysterious "white house," and the death pit worked to full capacity.

Ten transports arrived daily. There were not enough workers to carry all the luggage, so it was piled in mountainous heaps and remained there at the station for days.

An extra shift of Sonderkommandos was added. Still it was not enough. At last four hundred Greeks from the Corfu and Athens transport were ordered in the Sonderkommando. Now, something truly unusual happened. These four hundred demonstrated that in spite of the barbed wire and the lash they were not slaves but human beings. With rare dignity, the Greeks refused to kill the Hungarians! They declared that they preferred to die themselves first. Sadly enough, they did. The Germans saw to that. But what a demonstration of courage and character these Greek peasants had given. A pity the world does not know more about them!

With so many extra souls to be liquidated, the extermination facilities were literally swamped. Additional buildings had to be used as gas chambers. Big ditches were dug, filled with bodies, and covered with wood. There was no time to waste. People who were not quite dead from the gas were also thrown into the ditches, and burned with the others. German efficiency.

This mass extermination was undertaken with the active complicity of the pro-German Hungarian government. Indeed, Hungary was the only country to send official commissions into the camps to come to agreement with the administration on the rate and speed of deportation. The Fascist authorities in Budapest cooperated by escorting their deportees by Hungarian policemen, a step which no other European government ever took no matter how collaborationist its policies.

The arrival of the Hungarian policemen at Auschwitz, which I witnessed, caused an unbelievable scene. Hungarian deportees who had arrived on earlier trains caught sight of those uniforms and cheered. They were so homesick that they ran to the barbed wire and showed their great joy by singing and sobbing, and finally, by joining in their national anthem. Did they think that the police had come to rescue them? A tragicomic drama,

114

for the guests they acclaimed with such fervor had come to deliver their comrades to the Nazi S.S. Had not the camp guards intervened, these patriots would have smothered their dear countrymen in their arms. A few lashes of the whip and a few revolver shots tore them from the policemen whose helmets, surmounted with rooster feathers, had reminded the internees of the Hungarian plains and of the hills of Buda overlooking the silvery waters of the Danube.

CHAPTER XVII

The Methods and Their Madness

Auschwitz was a work camp, while Birkenau was an extermination camp. But there were a few work kommandos at Birkenau
for various manual tasks. I was forced to participate in most of
these squads, at one time or another.

First, there was the "Esskommando," that is, the food-carriers.
After the morning roll call, I went to the kitchens with my
companions to take the pots of food. We had to carry them to
the hospital about half a mile away. At least that was useful
work, and one could only complain that it was fatiguing.

There were some tasks that were perfectly useless. We were
almost convinced that a madman set upon driving everyone
else insane had thought them up. For example, we were
ordered to carry a heap of stones from one spot to another.
Each internee had two pails to fill to the brim. Then we
trudged several hundred yards more and emptied them. We
had to carry out this stupid assignment conscientiously. Once
the pile of stones had been removed, we breathed relief, hoping
that now we would have something more sensible to do.
Imagine our feelings when we were ordered to pick up the
stones and take them back to their original place! Apparently
our masters wanted us to repeat the classic task of Sysiphus.

Sometimes, instead of the stones, we had to carry bricks, or
even mud. These assignments seemed to have but one purpose:
to break our physical and moral resistance and render us candi-

dates for the selections.

Once, I was ordered to the "Scheisskommando," or the latrine cleaning squad. Equipped with two buckets we arrived each morning at the pit behind the hospital. We drew up full pails of the excrement and carried them a few hundred yards away to another pit. So it went on all day. Finally, dead from nausea and disgust, we washed as well as we could and went to bed, knowing that tomorrow we would have to repeat our performance.

The odor which reeked from my co-worker in the Scheisskommando, who slept beside me, literally made me sick. I must have had the same effect on her.

There was also the mud. Auschwitz-Birkenau was situated on a marshy terrain, and the mud never disappeared. It was a sly and powerful enemy. It penetrated our shoes, our clothing, and even soaked through our soles, which came off and made our swollen feet even heavier. When it rained, the camp was transformed into an ocean of mud, paralyzing traffic and making every task unbelievably difficult. Mud and the crematory — these were our greatest obsessions.

Certain kommandos worked outside the camp. These were in the "Aussenkommando." They left early in the morning, no matter what the weather was. Members of these squads had to do their work on an empty stomach, with no food whatever except that yellowish liquid which the cooks called tea or coffee, as they pleased. The departure of these prisoners, some dressed in ragged evening dresses, others in pajamas with convict stripes, in wooden shoes or unmatched boots, was a heart-rending spectacle. Shivering in the cold of the dawn, their teeth chattering, their cheeks wet with tears, they were forced to sing as they marched. What joy could one find in singing in Auschwitz! But they had to march in step and not leave the ranks, for the ferocious police dogs of the S.S., trained by the German system, jumped at the throats of those who strayed from the column or fell behind.

117

The work in the fields was very exhausting. Our overseers kept close watch to see that none of us paused to catch our breaths. Stragglers were always beaten with whips and clubs.

If, at the end of her strength, an internee fainted, she was hit with a bludgeon to revive her. If that would not do it her skull was literally crushed with a club or with boot kicks. Thereafter she no longer had to appear at the roll call.

Fainting was quite common because the kommandos always included sick persons. I saw women who were stricken with pneumonia painfully walking the eight miles from the camp to the place of work and digging all day to avoid being sent to the hospital. They knew only too well that the hospital was only an antechamber for the crematory. Besides, even those who were willing to go to the hospital could not always do so. To be admitted one had to have a very high fever. It is easy to understand why the internees died like flies during the wet and cold months.

Once, when we left the fields, an S.S. armed with a whip stopped us to question a female "Musulman." "How long have you been here?" he shouted.

"For six months," replied the poor woman. She had been a professor in civilian life, but she dared not raise her eyes to the S.S., who had formerly been her hairdresser.

"We have to punish you," the German declared forcefully. "You have no sense of discipline. A 'correct' prisoner would have been dead three months ago. You are three months too late, you miserable slut!" With that he whipped her until she was unconscious.

When any internees collapsed either from the work, or because of the beatings by the S.S., we had a special duty to carry the body back to the camp. For it was absolutely imperative that the entire column be complete at the last roll call. Those were the rules.

Our funeral procession was welcomed to the camp by the internees' orchestra playing gay tunes at the entrance. For the

118

rules decreed that a spirit of gaiety should prevail at the end of the workday.

*   *   *   *

From time to time, the Germans disinfected the camp. Executed rationally this measure would have contributed to the betterment of our hygienic conditions. But, like everything else at Auschwitz-Birkenau, the disinfection was carried out in a mocking fashion and only increased our mortality rate. That was doubtless part of the idea.

The disinfection began with the isolation of four or five barracks. We had to present ourselves by barracks at the washroom. Our clothing and shoes, items that had been acquired at the cost of great privations, were taken away and placed in a fumigating oven, while we passed under a shower.

The operation lasted only a minute, not long enough to get clean at all. Then, after being doused with a disinfectant on the head and the parts of the body covered with hair, we were moved to the exit. Those who had lice had their hair clipped again.

But, after leaving the washroom, we had to line up outside completely naked, regardless of the season or the weather. We had to wait until the line was perfectly formed, though it often took more than an hour. If we caught pneumonia, very well.

Shivering, we finally returned to our barracks. Those who had hoped to warm themselves realized again that Birkenau was no place to be an optimist. For while we were gone the few blankets had been taken away. We could only wait until they were restored. The administration was in no hurry. We continued to shiver on the bare boards of the koias.

At last, they returned our clothing. Even this was not done without deception. They never returned all they had taken. Once, for example, fourteen hundred women were disinfected, but only enough clothing for twelve hundred was returned to us.

119

The two hundred unfortunate women whose clothes had disappeared had no other recourse than to "organization." While they waited they had only a few blankets in which to keep warm.

As I mentioned before, there was only one blanket for ten women, so bitter fighting broke out among those who had to share a single blanket. Besides, each felt that she had the right to wear it during the day.

Women who had no clothes and could not obtain blankets had to come to the roll call completely naked. It was impossible to remain in the barracks and not appear for the roll call.

The S.S. guards knew why our fellow inmates appeared naked. But they always beat those "treacherous" females who were so shameless. And the administration liquidated the naked first.

We did everything in our power to help those poor creatures, but we had little clothing to give away. One woman took off her slip, another gave a pair of drawers, still another a brassiere. One inmate had nothing to wear for days except a blouse which covered only her arms and shoulders.

In our distress, L. rendered us invaluable services. His friend in the clothing storehouse, "organized" three or four blouses each day, and as many pairs of drawers. But the "organization," however active, was not enough to meet our needs.

After each disinfection, the barracks were visibly less crowded. The corpses were laid out behind the barracks, to the great joy of the rats, who were surely the happiest occupants of Auschwitz-Birkenau. These rodents, fattening on the dead flesh of our unfortunate companions, were so much at home that nothing we could do would drive them from the barracks. They were not afraid of us. Quite the contrary. They may have felt that *they* were the real masters.

* * * *

My captivity, like that of other internees, was marked by

several "changes of residence." I had to move to three different camps, and my work was changed countless times. Most often I worked in the health service, at the infirmary or the hospital, but I was also charged with menial tasks such as latrine cleaning and labor in the fields. A caprice of the blocova or a chance evacuation was enough to change my situation from one extreme to another. At the end of autumn, 1944, I was on the latrine squad and only by a stroke of luck was I able to return to the hospital shortly thereafter.

At the beginning of December, 1944, only two women's camps remained. The others had either been evacuated or their inmates exterminated. These were B-2, a work camp; and E, formerly for Gypsies, but which now included the hospital blocks.

The internees at B-2 worked in the weaving mills where detonator fuses were manufactured. Conditions there were miserable. The workers spent the day in blocks that were filled with mounds of dirty wool, one or two yards high. The slightest stir raised whirlpools of dust that clogged the nostrils and choked the lungs. Without water, they could not even dream of washing. Little wonder then that the hospital was crowded with internees from B-2.

Twice a week the sick women from the weaving mill were taken to Camp E. Those who could no longer walk were brought in trucks or wheelbarrows, the rest crawled and held one another up. I could not help but think of the lame leading the blind. Because of a stupid rule, the sick, no matter how seriously ill, had to go under the showers before being hospitalized. Often they fainted. Sometimes we dared to ignore the inhuman rule and took the suffering women directly to the hospital.

Since it was always filled, conditions at the hospital were almost intolerable. Malnutrition and epidemics brought as much as 30 per cent of the total number of internees to us. Two or three, frequently four, patients had to share one berth. Pressed against each other, they felt the sufferings of their neighbors as well as their own. Instead of being cured, a patient might contract a new disease in the hospital. Because of the close quarters it was impossible to fight contagion.

This dreadful place certainly offered a rich field for observation of the pathology of malnutrition. Oedema, phlegmon, panaris, and that form of persistent diarrhea which the Germans called "Durchfall," the furunculosis, extreme manifestations of vitamin deficiencies, and finally pneumonia, were the most common phenomena. We also had contagious cases of diphtheria, scarlet fever, and typhus, which was propagated by the myriads of lice with which the camp abounded.

A merciless war was waged between the lice and the internees, with the parasites generally the victors. The ludicrous disinfections could not discourage our adversaries, and we had neither the time nor the strength to struggle against a foe that multiplied at so bewildering a rate. We were all infested: those who worked in the kommandos, those who remained in the barracks, and those who were in the hospital. The lice were everywhere: in the clothing, in the koias, in the hair, in the beards, even in the eyebrows. They even crept under the bandages of the sick, covering the skin. I often told myself that if we remained in the camp much longer, we would all be dead, leaving only the rats and the lice.

In the last months of our stay at Camp E, there was some improvement. The Lageraelteste (little Orli), fought the lice without mercy. She took the clothing from the internees and left them to die of exposure, rather that let the parasites breed.

In the struggle against vermin we who worked in the hospital were relatively privileged. We were somewhat less crowded in our dormitory, and we had the precious wash basin with the holes in it. Besides we dared not abandon the field to the pests, for we were constantly exposed to them and at each examination the sick "passed over" an abundance to us.

122

We had daily delousing sessions and never ceased to encourage the patients to do likewise. Had there been more of us, and had we been better equipped, the lice would never have ruled. We knew that we failed, and suffered deeply because of it.

No spectacle was more comforting than that provided by the women when they undertook to cleanse themselves thoroughly in the evening. They passed the single scrubbing brush to one another with a firm determination to resist the dirt and the lice. That was our only way of waging war against the parasites, against our jailers, and against every force that made us its victims.

*   *   *   *

All the internees of Auschwitz-Birkenau had one dream, *to escape*: Hundreds of thousands of deportees entered these camps, but the number of those who succeeded in leaving of their own free will was infinitesimal. During my whole stay, I heard of no more than four or five escapes that had gone well. Even in these cases, the results were not completely sure.

The German system was frighteningly effective. The guards were rewarded for shooting escaped prisoners. First, there was the barbed wire with its high-tension current. Then there were the "Miradors," the dogs outside, who had been specially trained to run down fugitives. Besides, the moment someone was missing a strict set of measures were put into effect. A siren wailed. When we heard this fearful sound piercing the air, we knew what it meant: someone had tried to save herself. We trembled and prayed for her success. Our sentiments were mixed with selfishness, for we hoped that whoever escaped from the inferno would tell the world what was happening at Birkenau, that someone might come to our aid at last. If the Allies could blow up the crematory oven! The pace of the extermination would at least be slowed.

But the chase began without a minute lost. At night, powerful searchlights probed the surrounding areas, and patrols accompanied by police dogs prowled the region. Unfortunately the fugitive could not even count on the aid of the natives. Three or four days' hunger and thirst generally conquered those who had, by some miracle, succeeded in escaping the pursuers. It was, of course, impractical for them to enter any city to seek food until they had changed their rags for a less noticeable garb.

There was virtually no chance to escape without the cooperation of the guards. Several deportees who had been there for a long time and had procured gold or precious stones from "Canada," did succeed in bribing a guard. A few got hold of S.S. uniforms. But even such precautions did not assure success.

In the summer of 1944, an Aryan Polish worker who labored in section B-3 succeeded in getting two S.S. outfits, one for himself and the other for a Jewish girl from Poland, with whom he was in love. Both had been here for a long time. They escaped from Birkenau through Auschwitz and reached the village of Auschwitz. There they spent two happy weeks, a real honeymoon after so many years of captivity. They felt so secure in their S.S. uniforms that they relaxed their vigil and began to stroll through the streets of the village. An S.S. officer remarked an irregularity in the appearance of the woman, and at once demanded to see their papers. Naturally, they were both arrested.

The rules provided that fugitives returned to camp must suffer an exemplary punishment in the presence of all the inmates. First, they were compelled to make the rounds of the camp carrying a placard listing the crime for which they were sentenced. Then they were hanged in the middle of the camp or sent to the gas chamber.

The Polish worker and his companion showed great courage. In front of the assembled crowd of internees, the girl emphatically refused to carry the placard!

The Germans behaved as though thunderstruck. An S.S.

124

guard beat her brutally. Then something unbelievable happened. Gathering all her strength, the girl struck her torturer in the face with her fist.

A murmur of astonishment ran through the assembly. Someone had struck back! Fuming with rage, the Germans threw themselves on the girl. A shower of blows and kicks felled her. Her face was covered with blood and her limbs were broken.

Triumphantly the S.S. chief slung over her body the sign which she had refused to carry. A truck appeared to fetch her. She was thrown into it as if she were a sack of flour. Still the girl, half dead, with a pierced eye and a gory face, raised herself and cried out: "Courage friends! They will pay! Liberation is near!"

Two Germans climbed into the vehicle and stamped on her. They achieved the silence they wanted, but they were still kicking her when the truck moved away.

Some time later, I was making an inspection of the infirmary during the rest hour. To my surprise, Tadek, the young, blue-eyed Pole whom I mentioned earlier, came in. However, it was not the same Tadek who had proposed to me in the washroom three months earlier. This man was a broken creature, thin, pale, and feeble.

Without a greeting, he sat down. Abruptly he declared, "I am planning to try to escape tomorrow. Everything is ready. I've thought of nothing else all these years. Maybe I'll be successful, but more likely I shall be caught and shot. I don't really care. I can't stand it any longer."

He paused. "Before I leave, I want to tell you that when I proposed to you, I was not sick. Before the war, I was a university professor in Warsaw. If you ever get out of the camp look for me there and I shall look for you in Transylvania." He enunciated each word clearly, adding, "Anyway, you cannot hate me any more than I hate and abominate myself."

He went to the door, but suddenly turned. In his eyes I

caught an expression of that same humaneness that I thought
I had recognized in his voice so long ago.

A few days later, Tadek's neighbors who were working in
our camp told me that he and his younger brother had escaped.
They had foiled all the guards and had reached "no man's
land," about a mile from the Russian lines. They were suffering
horribly from thirst, for they had not had a mouthful of water
in forty-eight hours. When they passed by a well, Tadek
stopped. His brother continued on. Tadek was quenching his
thirst when a German patrol sighted him. He was arrested.
Realizing that he was lost, he avoided the direction in which his
brother had gone for fear of betraying him. The brother succeeded in getting away, but Tadek was taken back to the camp
and put into a bunker.

The bunkers were penitentiary cells sunken into the ground.
They afforded neither air nor light, and were so small that the
prisoners had to stand up in them all night. During the day
they were taken out to do the most loathsome work on reduced rations. He had six and a half ounces of bread in three
days, and that was all.

After three or four days, the strongest of men would be sub-
dued. Tadek endured this treatment for many weeks. When
they finally decided to kill him, there was nothing left of the
human being I had known.

*   *   *   *

As the borders of the Greater Reich narrowed under the blows
of the Allies, the Germans evacuated the camps that were menaced by the advances. For this reason the occupants of a number of camps were evacuated to Auschwitz. When its turn
came, Auschwitz was to be transferred to the interior of the
Reich.

The internees from the Brassov camp in Poland were the
first to be transported to Auschwitz. The newly arrived were

126

assigned to B-2, the former Czech Camp. They lost many of their number during the journey. Many women "volunteers" had been confined at Brassov. Some earned fair livelihoods, and used their camp neighbors, the internees, to do their washing, mending, and cleaning. With the few coins they got from the "volunteers," the internees eased their hard lot by buying supplementary items at the canteen. There were no wonders there, but this little market was much appreciated. Besides, Brassov had been a work camp with a spinning mill in operation, and not an extermination camp. These internees knew nothing of crematory ovens. There the Germans had used their machine guns in the neighboring forests for mass executions of Russian, Polish, and French prisoners.

The evacuation of Brassov was accomplished in a hurry. The roll was called in the middle of the day. The internees were taken to railroad cars into which they were piled like animals. The internees who had been working outside the camp had a stroke of good fortune. When they returned that evening, they were welcomed by the Soviet troops who had just occupied the region.

Among the evacuees stranded at Auschwitz because of military operations was a large contingent of Jews from the ghetto of Lodz. Thanks to a Polish woman doctor, I was able to get an accurate picture of the life in that city during its occupation.

The ghetto was surrounded by a large water-filled ditch beyond which the German soldiers mounted guard with machine guns. Within the enclosure the Jews might circulate freely at certain hours, but most of the time they were compelled to work for the Wehrmacht. They manufactured S.S. uniforms and embroidered uniform-collars with the famous death's-head insignias. Their sick were cared for by their own doctors. The food in the ghetto was abominable and the mortality rate was extremely high.

The evacuation of this ghetto was also carried out by surprise. Once more the Germans resorted to their hypocritical methods

127

to save manpower. A large number of the men were seized and led to the station. When the desperate wives and mothers made inquiries, they were informed that the men were leaving to work in Germany and that women could accompany them. It is not necessary to repeat how the Jewish women of Lodz and their children rushed to the station, carrying with them whatever was most precious. The Germans filmed the scene and showed it in the newsreels to contradict the rumors that they ever used coercion!

The men, women, and children of the Lodz ghetto were now in extermination camps, notably at Birkenau.

I had to care for a number of them at the infirmary. They were in a deplorable physical condition, and their morale had sunk to a low ebb. Of all the sick, I dare say they were the most delicate and the least able to resist pain; next came the Greeks, the Italians, the Yugoslavs, the Dutch, the Hungarians, and the Rumanians. The most stoic of all, at least as far as I could determine, were the French and the Russians.

*   *   *   *

Internees from the East were not the only newcomers. We also received large numbers of resisters and other "undesirables" from the West. In September, 1944, before the liberation of the Lowlands, many Belgians arrived. The Jews from Teresienstadt also came. On the daily deportation trains came Greeks and Italians. The latter had spent time in the prisons of the peninsula; as the Allies advanced, the prisons were emptied and their occupants were dispatched to Birkenau. Their morale already undermined, most of these old prisoners had difficulty adapting themselves to the camp conditions. Among them suicides were frequent.

These arrivals caused changes inside the camp. More than ever, Birkenau became a real "Tower of Babel," with every kind of language spoken and diversified customs practiced. The only

128

"stable" element were the old "Schutzhaftling," officials of the camp, who oppressed the newcomers cruelly. They were truly the docile servants of the German State.

Birkenau also received internees from the nearby work camps who were no longer of any use to the German war machine. Auschwitz-Birkenau used to send the most robust of the internees to the region of Ravensbruck where there were many armament factories. Those who fell ill were sent back under the pretext that they needed medical attention. They were really weakened and dispirited and had no desire to survive.

The bodies of those who were executed in the nearby camps were also sent to Birkenau. Our crematory ovens served a vast region indeed. The German preference for incineration was surely not due to hygienic considerations; it saved burial and allowed them to make the most thorough reclamation of precious materials.

Some trains arrived at Birkenau, having departed — from Birkenau! One day it was announced that a train would take internees to Germany to work in the factories. All this took place as though it were an everyday occurrence. The deportees boarded the cars without even being jostled very much. The train started to move, executed a few maneuvers, left the station, and departed for an unknown destination. After a few hours, the same train returned — with the same passengers — to Birkenau, and the deportees were taken directly to the crematory ovens.

Why did the Germans resort to such complicated maneuvers? Was this operation made according to plan, or was it the result of the administrative confusion? In any case, the facts which I report are accurate in every detail.

Another day, a second train of deportees left for "work in a German factory." Days later the disinfection service of the camp turned back a considerable quantity of clothing, the property of our former companions. They had departed not for Germany but from this world. No one knew where or under

129

what circumstances those poor souls had been executed.

*   *   *   *

Despite the mass arrivals, the number of internees continued to dwindle. One reason was that after autumn, 1944, many were actually transferred to factories to replace German workers who had been sent to the front. The German criminals of the camp, who wore the green triangle, were offered their liberty if they would fight the enemies of the Reich. The majority of the S.S. left for the front; those who remained were chiefly invalids for whom the service at Auschwitz was a rest cure after combat.

The selections also thinned our ranks. One horrible rainy afternoon a detachment of S.S. arrived at the infirmary. Using strong arm tactics, as was their habit, they made sixty sick women assemble under the portal of the hospital. The patients were ordered to throw all their possessions into a heap, even their meager daily rations and the hospital shirts. Not motor vehicles but garbage carts were sent for this group of unfortunates. The cortege moved out in a drumming rain, in the midst of the ocean of mud which covered the soil of Birkenau. Not a cry arose from the victims. They bade us good-bye with resigned gestures that seemed to say, "Today it is our turn, tomorrow it will be yours."

An hour later the garbage carts returned from the direction of the crematories. This time, the carts were empty.

Birkenau was in the process of full scale liquidation. For the administration perceived that it would be necessary to evacuate before the advancing Russians. Even the crematory ovens must be destroyed to leave as few traces as possible.

However, the liquidation was carried out slowly and methodically. The Sonderkommandos were instructed to destroy one oven at a time. All the others continued to function, and some were still consuming bodies as late as December, 1944.

130

New trains continued to arrive, but the newcomers were selected at the station. The selectionees were sent directly to the gas chamber, while the others were sent on toward the interior of Germany. However, in some instances, entire trainloads were exterminated immediately upon arrival at Birkenau. What caprice determined it, I could not say.

At this time my duties occasionally brought me near the station. One day, with a few companions, I saw a train crowded with Russian civilians whom the Germans had apparently taken along in their retreat. The car doors were open. Inside, children were crying and old folks were groaning, while a few young people swaggered and sang Russian chants. At the sight of us, the women peered through the door, begging for a little water or a piece of bread. *"Woda . . . . khleb."* Two words identified them as Russian. We had heard that so often, we knew "bread and water" in all the languages of Europe.

They asked where they were. They could not suspect that they had reached the end of their "voyage."

I returned to the camp much depressed. As was the case nearly every time a new train of selectionees came to the station, the internees were confined to their respective barracks. Only the members of the infirmary staff had the right to circulate. My white blouse served as a temporary safe-conduct badge.

The next day I went to the station again. There was no one at the doors. The cars had been emptied during the night. No one had seen the Russians in the camp. In the following days other trains arrived, and the fate of these people was settled in the same manner.

Another recollection continued to haunt me. Under the surveillance of the guards, I was driven to Camp F.K.L., with a group of internees. Near the station we had to stop to let a column of deportees pass. These were middle-class Poles, judging from their features and from their clothing. I recognized some as railroad men, rapid transit workers, postmen, nuns, and schoolboys. They were not marching fast enough to suit the guards, so the latter spurred them on with clubs and whips and revolver shots.

Suddenly, a man about sixty years old in postman's uniform lost his balance and fell. A youth of about eighteen tried to help him get up. The old man was trying to rise when an S.S. came up and with one revolver shot coolly slaughtered him.

I stood about three yards away with my neighbors.

I cannot describe the look that the dying man fixed on the youth who had sought to save him. Nor can I suggest the despair and grief in the young man's voice as he cried, "Oh, father!"

Meanwhile, the S.S. assassin took out his pocket lighter and tried to light a cigarette. He carefully protected the flame from the wind. The breeze was strong and he had to try many times. It was certainly easier for him to destroy a human life than to light a cigarette. Finally, his cigarette glowed and the S.S. put his lighter into his tunic. Only then did he see the young man sobbing over the body of his mortally wounded father.

"Weiter gehen!" (Get going!) shouted the S.S. As the young man did not seem to hear, he lashed him with his whip. One, two, three strokes delivered in fury. The youth rose painfully, gazing for the last time at his dying father. Still reeling under the blows, he took his place again in the column which was being beaten toward the forest of Birkenau.

CHAPTER XVIII

Our Private Lives

For six months I shared the minute space of Room 13 with five persons. Dr. "G." was, perhaps, the most interesting of my companions. She was a doctor from Transylvania who, to an extent that was positively unhealthy, refused to reconcile herself to the fact that she was no longer living her old life of pre-Auschwitz days. Every evening she informed us that the blocova had invited her to tea, and described the incident as though it were one of those elegant tea parties she had known before the war.

We knew what the "tea party" had been. What kind of tea could anyone have in this place? But the doctor insisted upon embellishing and glamorizing everything about her. Thus she lived in a separate dreamworld of her own creation.

My second companion was a blonde Yugoslav girl. She pretended to be a doctor, but to the rest of us in the infirmary she was nothing of the kind; at best, she might have been a first-year medical student. She did not dare to apply a bandage and trembled that the Germans would discover that she had lied. Then she would end up in the crematory as had others who had falsely declared themselves to be physicians. Whenever she could lay hands on some popular book dealing with medicine, she would study voraciously. Real medical books were not available. The only ones around were "medical advisers" for family use. The truth was that the elementary knowledge she

133

possessed was enough in surroundings where proper medical treatment was impossible anyway. Later she was assigned to the hospital for contagious diseases. There she might have done a lot of harm, for she could not differentiate between the maladies. And she was the *chief* doctor in our camp hospital, whose instructions we *had* to follow.

My third companion was Doctor Rozsa, a Czech pediatrician, a real doctor. She worked enthusiastically and was faithful to her calling. She was a short, ugly woman of about fifty-five. It was moving to hear her speak in youthful, eager terms of her great lover back home. One day an acquaintance who had known her before Auschwitz came in. The guest spoke admiringly of the wonderful work the doctor had done in the past. When Dr. Rozsa was called out, and we remained alone with her friend, we asked her — woman fashion — to tell us about the doctor's romance. We learned that the poor woman's love was entirely one-sided, the object of it was probably unaware of her existence. But this passion was a form of escape for her, in the same way that Dr. G.'s dreamworld was.

My fourth roommate I shall call "S." She was a first-class surgeon, who had formerly been my husband's chief assistant. She had been brought to the camp in company with her four sisters, and was a real martyr to sisterly affection. The sisters were in the camp as ordinary prisoners, and suffered every privation of concentration camp life. S. lived only for them; their fate was on her mind every hour of the day.

The fifth in our group was a dentist. She had been married just before the deportation order and had been brought away with her husband. As she said whimsically, "We spent our wedding night in the freight car."

Later on, seven of us lived in the same cubbyhole. The seventh was Magda, a warm-hearted creature who was a chemist by profession. She was the one "selected" for liquidation at the same time that I was. We had both escaped that fate and felt close to each other. Magda shared the dentist's narrow bunk. I had a bed-mate too, Lujza, also the wife of a doctor. We slept at opposite ends of the bunk, for we would not have fitted in otherwise. Our chief problem was to avoid pushing each other off the narrow plank while we were sleeping; ours was the highest tier.

Borka, another Yugoslav girl of about twenty-two, was one of the most unselfish persons I have ever met. She added the domestic touch in our room and cleaned up after us.

Another roommate, Dr. "O." was the precise opposite of Dr. G. The latter created a pleasant dreamworld, but Dr. O. always saw things worse than they actually were. We often wondered if she had been born a pessimist, or whether the camp had made her one.

Eventually, twelve women shared the tiny room. It was airless and uncomfortable, but we thought it a paradise, because it was apart from the rest of the camp, and we had a minute degree of privacy in it.

We medical workers were always together, at night in the small cubbyhole in Barrack 13; during the day in the infirmary. We knew what there was to know about one another; we laughed together and we cried together. Naturally, we had our differences of opinion. Our conflicts usually arose from insignificant causes.

We had no chairs. The only places to sit were on the two lower bunks, the beds of Dr. G. and the dentist. These two intelligent women, who probably had been excellent housewives, sobbed like children if we sat on their beds. In a way they were justified, because the infirmary was dirty and louse-ridden. We were exposed not only to our patients' illnesses, but their vermin as well.

Amazingly enough, none of us caught a serious infection, although there were few precautions we could take against germs. The itch was the only malady to which we were sensitive. I was constantly getting it from the patients. Indeed, I had it seven times. I made desperate efforts to get medicine to treat

135

it. I suffered as much from the itch as from the beatings. I could not sleep or work, and my whole body was covered with sores from the endless scratching. When I did get healing applications, my roommates protested against my using it at night. The salve had a horrible odor and made the room unbearable.

The ointment divided us into two factions. One group urged that I use the salve at night so that I could free myself of the torture; the other that I should use it only during the day, in the infirmary, where we had to endure many smells anyway, and the stench of the ointment did not matter. Later Magda and the dentist also fell prey to the itch, and the insupportable smell became ever-present in the room.

Every morning there was a general struggle for the use of the wash basin. After all, we were twelve. Borka, the little Yugoslav girl, had to fetch the water. Sometimes she arrived in tears. She could get so little water that it was not enough for drinking, to say nothing of washing.

We had no mirror. Still we could examine our reflections in the water, if we had water. When our hair began to grow, we saw that we had quite a few gray. Since we had neither brushes nor combs, we looked like untidy adolescents. Dr. G. declared we were an awesome sight. She prevailed upon one of her patients, a hairdresser who had a comb, to arrange our hair in return for two portions of bread.

My eyebrows caused me much suffering at the beginning. They were thin by nature, but in the camp they thought that I was still plucking them. Many unkind remarks were passed by my fellow-prisoners on this feature. Several times I was beaten by the Germans for the same reason. Finally, they realized that I had, indeed, come into the world with thin eyebrows. It was easier for me when everyone appreciated that and ceased to torment me, at least, on that score.

There were daily arguments over the "Pinkly," which was no more than a beggar bundle. "Pinkly" was a piece of rag, a sock or stocking, sometimes an old cap, tied into a sort of bag that

136

was our "hand-bag," "closet," and "pantry." The contents of a pinkly bundle gave a perfect picture of our poverty. Here each prisoner concealed her fortune; her margarine, her bread, and her coffee spoon of marmalade. The "wealthier" prisoners might have a toothless comb. A small tin box in the pinkly was an unmistakable sign of "prosperity."

"Pinklys," being luxuries, were forbidden. There was no place in the barrack where they could be secreted, during roll call, so we hid them beneath our skirts. Severe punishment — sometimes death — awaited anyone who let her pinkly fall while standing stiffly at attention. The betraying pinkly brought tragedy not only to its owner, but upon the rest too, for it would call for a search and the confiscation of our hard-won possessions.

When we moved into Room 13, the pinkly question was solved. There, too, we had to hide them in the most fantastic places so that they would not be discovered at inspection. When we heard in advance of an inspection, one of us would remove the pinklys ahead of time. But they were not safe even from the other prisoners. While we were in the infirmary, they would enter our room and steal our treasures. Dr. G., and the dentist, who were the richest, always complained about thefts.

Dr. Rozsa was the only one who never lost anything, for she did not own anything. She was a grownup child: at least she had no desire to amass "property."

Dr. G., who was a good doctor, tried to make her dreamworld real. She kept a "maid," a luxury only the blocovas were offered. Every morning, before Dr. G. got up, one of her patients came in, cleaned the doctor's shoes, tidied her clothes, and made her bed. Dr. G. even had a silk coverlet. To avoid our jealousy, she later got one for each of us; but they were ragged and of inferior quality. She was the only one of our group who did no washing, even in camp. Her white smock was washed by her "maid," and the blocova allowed her to have it pressed with her own iron.

137

Dr. G. was always trying on dresses. She got them on the black market or as gifts, and had them altered. Toward the end of our captivity, when we could hear the Russian guns, Dr. G. remarked, "Well, girls, the time has come for me to have a traveling costume made."

The pessimist said, "But my dear, they'll kill us."

"Suppose they don't?" the doctor returned. "Then here I'll be, without a traveling suit."

We laughed. Yet we were grateful to her. That intense femininity of hers provided us with many entertaining moments.

G.'s dresses grew in number, and L built us a closet from three planks. It was actually for Dr. G., for we needed no closet for our few miserable rags.

Of course, each prisoner was permitted only one dress. G. was therefore in a constant state to find new hiding places for her clothes. Poor thing, she was completely broken up when a pleated skirt, the best article in her wardrobe, was stolen from her straw mattress. Her blue raincoat, which she was saving for "going away," also disappeared. She could not eat all day from grief.

Officially, Dr. G. was the camp obstetrician and Dr. S. was the surgeon. G. took some of the surgical cases, and a dispute arose between the two physicians. Dr. S. asked for no thanks for her work. But Dr. G. needed praise to keep her dreamworld going. Although they were next door to the crematory and lived in constant terror of death, they kept up this senseless "competition."

However, we had a few genuinely unselfish souls. For example: the blonde Polish woman who, when I was about to leave Block 26 and go to Block 13, stood in the doorway and called me back. "You can't leave us like this. We must have a farewell supper."

"Farewell supper?" I asked. "What shall we use for food?"

"Yesterday I found a tube of toothpaste. We'll eat that," she replied.

138

So those of us who slept together squeezed into a corner of the koia and spread the tooth paste on bread. Does it sound mad to my readers? We prisoners in Auschwitz seldom had had a better meal than we enjoyed that night.

Despite the differences in Room 13, we liked one another, and frequently proved that we could make sacrifices for each other. Unfortunately, my companions could never forgive me the packages I received while I was in the infirmary. Even with the best intentions, I could give no reasonable explanation for them. We shared everything, even the most trifling acquisitions. Still, I was bound not to speak of these parcels. When they asked me, I had to give evasive answers.

That their imaginations were inflamed by my behavior was understandable. Lujza, who was my bed mate and best friend, told me that the others tried to guess the secret of those packages. I dared not tell even Lujza. Sometimes, when I could not immediately pass on a parcel, I kept it overnight, under my head. She would not have been willing to spend the night here had she known I hid explosives in our bed.

One evening they all insisted that I explain my furtive visitor and my secret journeys to various corners of the camp.

"What do these people want from you; and why, at the busiest times, do you so often disappear?"

I dared not tell them anything. They punished me by refusing to speak to me for several days, except in the infirmary when it was absolutely necessary.

Luckily my birthday arrived, and they forgave my closemouthedness as my birthday present.

I had another gift. L. brought me a used toothbrush from which the bristles had been worn off on one end; the prisoner from whom L. had bought it for three pieces of bread had used it for several months. My companions were astonished and delighted with this rare item. The little green apple which I received from a member of the underground also caused a sensation. A *real* apple.

CHAPTER XIX

The Beasts of Auschwitz

Of all the S.S. in our camp, Joseph Kramer, "the beast of Auschwitz and Belsen," who was Criminal No. 1 at the trial of Luneburg, achieved the greatest notoriety. But we inmates had little contact with him. As Commander-in-Chief of a large part of the camp, he rarely left the administration offices, and he appeared only at certain inspections or on special occasions.

It was said that Kramer had been a man of many trades. Once he had been a bookkeeper. He certainly kept the books on human lives at Auschwitz, for it was he who received the orders from Berlin on the rate of extermination.

Kramer was a robust figure. His brown hair was crew cut, his eyes were black and piercing. His hard, gloomy features were not easy to forget. His walk was heavy and ponderous, his manner deliberate and unperturbed. Everything about his bearing gave him a Buddha-like air.

I saw him once or twice at the station when selections were being made from the new transports. I also saw him on two other occasions under circumstances which are indelibly recorded in my memory. The first time was in the summer of 1944. I cannot recall the exact date, but it was the day after the thousands in the Czech Camp were liquidated.

"Everyone outside! Empty the barracks!" That order was shouted at the beginning of the afternoon. Work was suspended as we rushed to obey. We were assembled in the large clearing

140

in front of the barracks. Now, the Germans broke all precedents, for they authorized us to sit down together on the ground, an unheard of privilege. In the midst of the crowd of women were many men, deportees who worked in our camp and to whom it was generally forbidden to address a word.

Suddenly the camp orchestra appeared. The musicians, dressed in the striped uniforms of inmates, mounted the platform and began to play light music and dance tunes. My heart pounded. One wanted to relax and be gay, but I had been disappointed too often to believe in anything the Germans did.

What could be the meaning of this popular concert? While the orchestra played its "swing," I could hear echoes of the heart-rending cries of the Czech children who had but yesterday been murdered.

Unexpectedly, German airplanes appeared over our heads. They circled so low that they threatened to shear off the roofs of the barracks. Then I understood. We were being filmed! They were undoubtedly preparing a "documentary" on the idyllic existence in the Nazi concentration camps. What would they show the world? Inmates of both sexes taking a sun bath outside their barracks while they listened to jazz music! What a windfall for the German propaganda machine which was seeking to combat the atrocity stories already current in the Western press.

A beaming smile on his lips, Kramer, the commander of the camp, suddenly passed among us. Perhaps he was being photographed as our genial host at this "rest haven." The whole mock drama was apparently his work.

Months passed. As the Red Army advanced further on the Polish plains, hope began to flourish anew in our hearts.

Those who saw Herr Kramer in the course of his inspections reported that he seemed to be more and more anxious. One day he issued the following order: "Camp No. 1 must be liquidated tomorrow at noon. It must be completely empty for inspection. Signed: Kramer."

141

The number of internees had already been reduced, but we still had about 20,000 women. To transfer such a large number of deportees into Germany in so short a time was almost impossible. Yet Kramer's order was executed in the required period.

By the next afternoon nothing remained in No. 1, except the hospital with its thousand patients and the hospital personnel, including those of us in the infirmary. We had no illusion about the fate that awaited either our patients or ourselves.

When the day's work was ended we retired to our room, which was at this time in the former urinal of Barrack 13. None of us thought of sleep. I took the most precious of my treasures from their hiding places. I found a candle which I had been saving for a great occasion, and lit the wick.

In the feeble glimmer of that light, we spent a sleepless night, all thinking of the same thing, the death that was concealed across the threshold of the coming dawn. Although the wind blew in through the cracked windowpanes, we thought that we would suffocate. "Enemy" planes flew overhead. The eerie wail of sirens went through the camp. Finally, the pale day broke.

We arrived at the hospital. After a few moments, Dr. Mengerle appeared, followed by twenty S.S. guards. A few minutes later, Joseph Kramer strode in. Without replying to the greetings of his subordinates, the latter halted in the middle of the room, his legs apart, his hands behind his back. He barked orders to his lieutenant.

One of the ambulances that was used to take the victims to the gas chamber stopped in front of the hospital. Others followed it. Between the entrance to the hospital and the ambulances, the S.S. formed a cordon. Other S.S. directed the sick people to move out and into the vehicles.

Most of the patients were too weak to stand, but guards began to beat them with their truncheons and whips. A woman

142

who had not started to march was seized by the hair. In the fray, many women fell from the koias and fractured their skulls. My comrades and I had to stand by, mad with terror and impotent with rage, as we witnessed this horrible scene. A few of the sick women tried to escape or to resist, but the S.S. hurled themselves into the rows and beat them pitilessly. One can hardly describe it.

Then Kramer assigned us to a "medical" task. We were to remove the patients' blouses, the only clothing left to these poor women who had been chased from their beds and who were moaning from the lash. What reason could there be for such a request? The blouses were no more than rags. But one did not ask questions or seek reasons. I tried to escape this assignment. An S.S. slapped me with such force that everything reeled before my eyes, and I nearly fell over.

I shall never forget the looks filled with hatred and reproach as our patients cried at us, "You, too, have become our tormentors!" They were right. Because of Kramer, we, whose duty it was to mitigate their sufferings, took their last possessions, those flimsy blouses. My friend, Dr. K., from the hospital, trembled like a leaf. She took advantage of a moment of respite and hurried away to the infirmary. I followed her in time to wrest a syringe from her hands. She was filling it with poison to kill herself.

I cannot say exactly how many ambulances and trucks filled with the sick left for the crematory ovens that day. To this moment, I have only a confused recollection. I see it through a fog: what I see are those horrible S.S. troops in fits of destructive insanity, blindly beating the sick women, kicking the pregnant. Kramer himself had lost his calm. A strange gleam lurked in his small eyes, and he worked like a madman. I saw him throw himself at one unfortunate woman and with a single stroke of his truncheon, shatter her skull.

Blood, nothing but blood. Everywhere blood! On the floor, the walls, the S.S. uniforms, their boots. Finally, when the last

143

ambulance had left, Kramer ordered us to scrub the floor and get the room into decent condition. Strangely, he lingered and supervised that cleaning himself. We worked like automatons. Our ability to reflect, to understand, was destroyed. Our minds were occupied with only one thought: how soon would death come? As we gathered the scattered blankets, the basins, the instruments, and the blouses torn from the women, we knew it was our turn next.

But we were wrong. Dr. Mengerle, who was present, suddenly separated the health personnel into two groups. The first he sent to a work camp; the second, of which I was a member, to another hospital at Camp F.K.L. Though Camp No. 1 was closed, the extermination factory of Birkenau would continue to operate.

In the interim, Kramer had disappeared. He had gone back to the central administration offices, doubtless to elaborate new orders and counter-orders for the lives and deaths of the thousands of slaves in Birkenau.

*　　　*　　　*　　　*

At least one person was missing from the prisoner's dock at the trial of Luneburg where the leaders of the camps were taken to account for their frightful deeds. This man should have paid as Dr. Klein and Dr. Kramer paid. I refer to Dr. Mengerle, who was the chief doctor after Dr. Klein left. Of all these whom I saw "in action" at the camp, he was far and away the chief provider for the gas chamber and the crematory ovens.

Dr. Mengerle was a tall man. One could have called him handsome were it not for the expression of cruelty in his features. At the trial, he should have been placed beside Irma Griese, his ex-mistress, the "blonde angel." But Dr. Mengerle had caught typhus when the camp was liberated. While he was convalescing, he escaped.

He was a specialist at the "selections." He made the deported

144

doctors accompany him from barrack to barrack; during the inspections, all the exits were closed. He could show up suddenly at any hour, day or night, that pleased him. He arrived when we least expected him, always whistling operatic airs. Dr. Mengerle was a fervent lover of Wagner.

He did not waste too much time. He made the internees disrobe to the skin. Then they had to march before him with their arms in the air while he continued to whistle his Wagner. As the frightened women came forward, he pointed out with his thumb: to the left; to the right!

No medical considerations governed his decisions. They seemed to be entirely arbitrary. He was the tyrant from whose decisions there was no appeal. Why should he trouble to select on the basis of any method? Nor did the state of health have anything to do with his selections. At the end of the inspection, Dr. Mengerle decided which of the two groups, right or left, would go off to the gas chambers.

How we hated this charlatan! He profaned the very word, "science!" How we despised his detached, haughty air, his continual whistling, his absurd orders, his frigid cruelty! If ever I was tempted to kill, it was one day when Mengerle's brief case lay on the table, and I saw the contours of a revolver inside. He was carrying out a selection at the hospital. To seize the gun and slaughter the assassin would have been a matter of seconds. Why didn't I do it? Because I feared the punishment that would have followed? No, because I knew that individual acts of revolt always brought mass reprisals at Auschwitz. I think that others stifled similar desires for the same reason.

With all that, Dr. Mengerle was a coward. Those in the Schreibstube knew that he employed sickening ruses to escape service at the front. When the S.S. left the camp en masse, Mengerle found a "special mission" that made his presence at Birkenau indispensable. One day he came to the infirmary and declared that because of our negligence, the typhus epidemic had reached such proportions that the entire region of Auschwitz was menaced. Alas, typhus epidemics did rage in the camp, but at this time we had comparatively few victims. The same day he sent us a large quantity of serum and directed mass vaccinations. We worked from six o'clock in the morning, in front of the infirmary, because Dr. Mengerle had forbidden us to vaccinate inside. The weather was cold and fingers were numbed, but thousands of internees waited to be innoculated and we had to work without stopping, late into the night. Dr. Mengerle was pressed for time; he needed an impressive report to send off to Berlin as quickly as possible.

His behavior was fantastic. He accused us of sabotaging the vaccinations. So, following out his order, we suspended the vaccinations the next day. Immediately he went into a violent temper and accused us, once more, of new sabotage.

One morning he would reproach us for not seeing enough patients, although from four hundred to six hundred sick people came to the infirmary each day, and the next day, he would chide us for giving the sick too much care and wasting scarce medicines.

Another time, he decided that malaria had been brought into the camp by the Greeks and Italians. Under the pretext of curbing the disease, he sent thousands to the gas chamber. How happy we were when we could deceive him. Instead of sending the blood of malaria victims for analysis, we substituted the blood of healthy inmates.

The coward, so afraid of death himself, enjoyed making others afraid. When Dr. Gertrude Mosberg from Amsterdam pleaded for the life of her father, who was also a doctor and was being sent to the crematory, Mengerle said, "Your father is seventy years old. Don't you think he has lived long enough?"

On another occasion he stood before a sick woman and gazed at her sarcastically. "Have you ever been on the 'other side'?" he asked. "What is it like over there?"

The poor woman did not know what he meant. She shrugged "Don't worry," he continued. "You will know very soon!"

146

Only once did I see this man lose his poise. That was when he came face to face with Kramer, who had the stronger personality. The music-mad Dr. Mengerle, so sure of himself before impotent internees, trembled in the face of the "beast of Belsen."

What conception could Dr. Mengerle have had of the medical work he did in the camp? His experiments, lacking scientific value, were no more than foolish playing, and all his activities were full of contradictions. I saw him take every precaution during an accouchement, watching to see that all aseptic principles were rigorously observed and that the umbilical cord was cut with care. Half an hour later he sent the mother and child to the crematory oven. The same with the vaccinations against typhus or scarlet fever. He carried out a series of health measures on internees whom he meant to dispatch to the gas chamber.

*   *   *   *

Among the S.S. women, I knew Irma Griese best, not because of any personal wish, but because of circumstances beyond my control. The "blonde angel," as the press called her, inspired me to the most violent hatred I ever experienced.

It may seem strange to repeat it so often, but she was exceptionally beautiful. Her beauty was so effective that even though her daily visits meant roll call and selections for the gas chambers, the internees were completely entranced, gazing at her and murmuring, "How beautiful she is!" Were a novelist to compose such a scene, his readers would accuse him of the wildest imagination. But pages from real life are often more horrible than those in novels.

This twenty-two-year-old S.S. was conscious of the power of her beauty and neglected nothing that would enhance its charms. She spent hours grooming herself before her mirror and practiced the most seductive gestures. Wherever she went she brought the scent of rare perfume. Her hair was sprayed with a complete range of tantalizing odors: sometimes she blended her own concoctions. Her immoderate use of perfume was perhaps the supreme refinement of her cruelty. The internees, who had fallen to a state of physical degradation, inhaled these fragrances joyfully. By contrast, when she left us and the stale, sickening odor of burnt human flesh, which covered the camp like a blanket, crept over us again, the atmosphere became even more unbearable. Yet our "angel" with the golden tresses employed her beauty only to remind us of our horrible position.

Her clothes were equally refined in style. Indeed, her S.S. uniforms fitted her better than her civilian attire did. She was especially fond of a sky-blue pea-jacket which matched her eyes. With this outfit she wore a darker tie at the collar of her blouse. Her whip, which she used so freely, stuck out jauntily from the leg of her boot.

She had a well-stocked wardrobe. I knew her dressmaker well; before the war she had directed a famous establishment in Vienna. Now Irma never gave her a free moment. The poor woman had to work from morning until night with only a crust of bread as a reward. But for Irma there was never any shortage of material, even English textiles. The gas chambers supplied an abundance of shoes and clothing, and all the martyred countries of Europe contributed to her collection. Her closets were crammed with clothing from the finest houses of Paris, Vienna, Prague, Amsterdam, and Bucharest.

The "angel" with the pure face had many love affairs. In the camp, it was gossiped that Kramer and Dr. Mengerle were her chief lovers. But her greatest affair was with an S.S. engineer whom she frequently met in the evenings. So that she might return to her post at the required hour, she always left him in the middle of the night. Whenever he was in her company, she radiated pride. "Look!" she seemed to be saying as she looked at us, "This is my kingdom. I have the absolute power of life and death over this herd." She had this power, as she could demonstrate when making her selections.

148

One day Irma entered our infirmary. With a curt order, she sent the sick patients from the room and went into conference with the surgeon, who was one of my best friends.

"I need your services," she declared briefly. "I have been told that you are very clever."

She explained exactly what was expected. The situation required delicate handling. It was dangerous to refuse anything to Irma Griese; yet if the superior authorities learned of her interference with nature, for it was an illegal operation, it would be just as dangerous for us.

My friend hesitated. Griese made tempting promises. "I will share my breakfast with you. You will have either wonderful chocolate or real coffee with milk. Cakes, too, and bread and butter!" Then she added, "I will also give you a winter coat, very warm."

However, the surgeon still was undecided. The danger was too great. Irma Griese flushed and produced her revolver. "I give you two minutes to make up your mind."

"I will do what you have asked," the doctor yielded.

"Very well! I will expect you tomorrow at five o'clock, Barrack 19. And mind you, I don't tolerate any lateness," the angel snapped, and left.

My friend was punctual. She asked me to go with her as a nurse. What a picture we saw! Irma Griese, the torturess, was actually sweating from fear. She trembled and groaned and was unable to control herself. She, who had coldly sent thousands of women to their deaths, and who brutalized them without a second thought, could not endure the slightest pain without whining.

No sooner was the operation over then she began to prattle.

"After the war, I intend to go into pictures. You will see my name in lights on the marqueé. I know life and I've seen a great deal. My experiences will be useful in my artistic career."

We were glad to be allowed to leave in peace. She could have had us killed right there. She had only to send us to the gas chambers and be done with us. I wonder why she did not.

Since those days, Irma Griese has indeed appeared in pictures. But not as she imagined she would. She was not the heroine of a love drama, nor did her beautiful face and figure decorate a screen. She appeared in the newreels at the time of the Luneberg trials. And when she was sentenced to die for her countless crimes, she did not hail death nor rush to embrace it. Her guards had to drag her to her execution. But what horrors that woman was guilty of before the day of judgment came!

*　　　*　　　*　　　*

Of all the S.S. chiefs I met, Dr. Fritz Klein puzzled me the most. He was a Saxon, originally from Transylvania. When the extermination factory was working at full speed, he was the medical director of the camp and one of the fervent zealots who ran the Nazi annihilation project. That he merited capital punishment a hundred times is an understatement. Yet, contrary to other S.S., Dr. Klein was, a "correct" assassin.

To be just, I must say that he was less sadistic than his colleagues. I had the impression that whatever he did, he, too, was a victim of circumstance. Perhaps he had a conscience. Anyway, he was the only S.S. butcher from whom I saw any humane reactions toward the deportees.

Perhaps I was impressed by his affability and the fact that sometimes he seemed sincerely interested in the sick people. Many internees were sensitive to such rare indications of benevolence.

He did not hesitate to send thousands of sick to the "hospital," but I also saw him save a few patients. One day a barrack doctor handed him a list of internees suspected of diphtheria. At the examination, the diagnosis was confirmed in two or three. But, after a rapid check, Dr. Klein sent the fourth away. "This is not a hospital case," he declared; "a common sore throat." Dr.

150

Mengerle, on the other hand, sent all the suspects to the hospital without troubling to examine anyone.

I have already related how Dr. Klein simulated anger against the infirmary and barrack doctors in order to have a pretext to spare several sick people from the selection. Another time he noted that a large number of selectionees were waiting in a washroom before being transferred to the "hospital."

"Why have they had to wait so long?" he asked the guard.

"The ambulance is not available," answered the S.S. "It is being used to transport the boxes!"

I knew that he was referring to the boxes of gas powder, which were always transported in the ambulance.

Dr. Klein's face darkened. "In that case, the selection was made too fast. It's not worth the trouble to keep these people here the whole day."

What sentiment caused such a reaction? Pity? Or was it simply indignation at the slovenly attitude of the guards?

Once again, while accompanying him on his rounds, I called attention to the fact that the internees had been standing before the barracks for many hours in a beating rain. He did not answer, but strode toward the place and ordered the inmates to return to their barracks.

Of Transylvanian origin, Dr. Klein often addressed me in my native tongue. He questioned me about my city and home. Once he asked me point-blank if I was not a member of the family of the noted doctor of the same town, who directed a sanatorium. He was referring to my husband, from whom I had not heard for weeks.

At the surge of memories I felt blind rage. How could I tell him the truth? Here I was, covered with mud, with shaved head, in rags, wearing two torn, mismated shoes. No, I was not the wife of a respected surgeon. I was a miserable creature trotting at the heels of an S.S. officer.

"No," I replied, gritting my teeth. "I don't know what you are talking about."

151

Dr. Klein was no fool. "Well, well, you don't say!" he said. "Incredible! But anyway," he added in a changed voice, "walk a few steps behind me. The rules of etiquette do not apply in this camp."

A few months later he paid a surprise visit to our infirmary and expressed a desire to visit the hospital.

I walked a few steps behind him as he had ordered me at our last meeting. He pointed to his bicycle and said, "My car had been taken away and we have no more gasoline! Listen! I am going to tell you something that will make you very happy. The war will be over shortly, and we shall all be able to go home again."

I looked around furtively. When I was with Klein, we were always surrounded by S.S. Fortunately no one was within earshot.

"I am very grateful," I said. "I have never heard an S.S. say anything like that."

"Oh, gratitude!" Dr. Klein shrugged, "I have no illusions. When the war is over, neither you nor the others will have the slightest regard for me."

Only at this moment did I catch a glimmer of his point of view. More clear-sighted than the others, he had surmised for a long time that the Germans had lost the war. His "benevolence" toward the inmates had been no more than simple calculation. Perhaps he was readying witnesses for the trials to come.

Besides Klein, I must mention Capezius, another Transylvanian. He had been one of the directors of the German Bayer Company in Transylvania.

The representatives of that firm had visited my husband frequently in our hospital in Cluj. At Christmas, we used to get perfumes, liqueurs, and medical books, all part of the process of wooing customers. Pencils advertising the Bayer name were always on our desks.

I had known Capezius before my captivity. Imagine then my

152

surprise when I found that he was a Hauptsturmfuehrer at Birkenau, and the powerful head of the pharmaceutical depots of the camps in the area. But we had few medicaments; my countryman was not too generous.

The Hauptsturmfuehrer frequently left the camp to "see his family" in Segesvar. After returning from one such visit, he appeared at our infirmary and spoke to Dr. Bohm, who had been deported from Capezius' community. "I was speaking to your brother two days ago in Segesvar. I promised him that I would take care of you."

The poor woman began to cry.

"I told him that you were very well," Capezius continued.

The doctor looked at her rags and was surprised at how "well" she was. Still she thanked the "benevolent" man. Some weeks later he came to the infirmary again and informed his protégé that the city had been occupied by the "enemy" and that her brother had become the mayor.

"If your brother takes good care of my family," he declared significantly, "you will see him again."

Soon Dr. Bohm was transferred from Birkenau to Auschwitz, where Capezius' headquarters were located. She was held as hostage, and we had no more news about her.

I am positive that Dr. Klein had the same intention in mind when he asked me if I had relatives in Transylvania. "In two days I am flying to Brasso. I would be willing to give any message to your family."

For a moment I was tempted. My sister-in-law lived there. But I remembered the incident of the postcards. It might be dangerous to give this murderer her address.

The same precaution kept me from asking Klein about my husband. I was afraid that instead of helping, I might endanger him if he were still alive. Experience had taught me always to be wary of "benevolence" from these Nazis.

CHAPTER XX

The Underground

Oppression as violent as that under which we lived automatically provokes resistance. Our entire existence in the camp was marked by it. When the employees of "Canada" detoured items destined for Germany to the benefit of their fellow internees, it was resistance. When laborers at the spinning mills dared to slacken their working pace, it was resistance. When at Christmas we organized a little "festival" under the noses of our masters, it was resistance. When, clandestinely, we passed letters from one camp to another, it was resistance. When we endeavored, and sometimes with success, to reunite two members of the same family — for example, by substituting one internee for another in a gang of stretcher bearers — it was resistance.

These were the principal manifestations of our underground activity. It was not prudent to go further. Yet there were many acts of rebellion. One day a selectee wrested a revolver from an S.S. and started to beat him with it. Desperate courage certainly expressed this gesture, but it had no effect except to bring mass reprisals. The Germans held us all guilty; "collective responsibility" they called it. The beatings and the gas chamber explain, in part, why the history of the camp includes few open revolts, even when mothers were forced to surrender their children to death. In December, 1944, the Russian and Polish internees had been ordered to give up their babies. The

154

order said they were to be "evacuated." Pitiful scenes followed: mothers distraught with grief hung crosses or improvised medals around the necks of their infants to be able to recognize them later. They shed bitter tears and abandoned themselves to despair. But there was no rebellion, not even suicide.

But an organized underground thrived. It sought to express itself in countless ways — from the broadcast of a "spoken newspaper," the sabotage practiced in the workshops devoted to war industries, and later to the destruction of the crematory oven by explosives.

The term "spoken newspaper" is perhaps presumptuous. We needed to disseminate war news that would help to bolster the morale of the internees. After solving technical problems of enormous difficulty, our friend, L., thanks to the cooperation of the "Canada," succeeded in constructing a little radio set! The radio was buried. Sometimes late at night a few trusted ones hurried out to listen to an Allied newscast. This news was then broadcast by word of mouth as fast as possible. The principal centers of our broadcasting were the latrines, which occupied the same "social" role that the washroom and the infirmary had in former times.

It was always interesting to observe the reactions of our overseers when such war news filtered to them, but hardly ever was it pleasant for us. The day after a heavy bombing of a German city, the Reich radio announced "reprisals." Wherever else the Reich sought revenge, they took it first in our camp with a monstrous selection. As for the guards, the continued defeats of the Wehrmacht made them more and more suspicious, and they multiplied the controls and searches. Even the chiefs grew nervous and preoccupied. Occasionally, Dr. Mengerle even forgot to whistle his operatic airs.

Some of the resisters in the camp sought to get word of our desperate situation to the Allies. We hoped that the Royal Air Force or the Soviet aviators would appear to destroy the crematory ovens, and that this, at least, would check the rate of the

155

extermination. A Czech internee, a former glazier and a militant leftist, did succeed in getting several reports to the Soviet Army.

There were some partisans in the region, and I understood that somehow they had established a contact with the camp. I was told that the explosive later used to destroy the crematory ovens was furnished by these guerrillas.

The parcels of explosive were no larger than two packs of cigarettes and could be easily hidden in a blouse. But how did the explosive enter the camp?

I heard that Russian guerrillas, hidden in the mountains, sent several of their number to the environs of Auschwitz. They reached a man from Auschwitz who worked outside the camp and who belonged to our underground. Those prisoners who worked in the fields dug the parcels from the earth where they had been concealed, and smuggled them inside.

Why had the explosives been sent? The aim was clear to all underground members — to blow up the dread crematory.

A few of the little parcels did fall into the hands of the S.S. That was almost unavoidable, and it provoked a brutal reaction. The gallows were put into use and bodies hung from them every day. Whenever the Germans suspected anything, a frenzied order was given: "Search the place!" and a group of S.S. rushed into our barracks.

They took everything apart and prodded every square inch of the camp, seeking other explosives. In spite of every precaution they took, our underground continued to exist and to function. The members changed, for the Germans decimated us without knowing whether we were underground or not; but the ideal remained unchanged.

A young boy who only a day before had accepted a package from me swung on the gallows. One of my comrades, numb with fright, whispered to me, "Tell me, isn't that the same boy who was in the infirmary yesterday?"

"No," I replied. "I have never seen him before."

That was the rule. Whoever fell was forgotten.

156

We were not heroes, and never claimed to be. We did not merit any Congressional Medals, Croix de Guerre, or Victoria Crosses. True, we undertook dangerous missions. But death and the so-called danger of death had a different meaning for us who lived in Auschwitz-Birkenau. Death was always with us, for we were always eligible for the daily selections. One nod might mean the end for any of us. To be late for roll call might mean only a slap in the face, or it might mean, if the S.S. became enraged, that he took out his Luger and shot you. As a matter of fact, the idea of death seeped into our blood. We would die, anyway, whatever happened. We would be gassed, we would be burned, we would be hanged, or we would be shot. The members of the underground at least knew that if they died, they would die fighting for something.

I have already mentioned that I served as a postbox for letters and parcels. One day I darted into the infirmary to slip a little package under the table. As I was doing this, an S.S. guard unexpectedly entered.

"What are you hiding there?" he inquired with a frown.

I think I grew white. I succeeded in taking hold of myself and replied. "I have just taken some cellulose. I'm putting the rest in order."

"Let's take a peek at this," cried the S.S., decidedly suspicious.

With trembling hands, I pulled a box of surgical dressings from under the table and showed it to him.

Luck was with me. He did not insist on going through the contents. He glared and went about his business. Had he searched the box, I should have been lost.

Often I had to accept letters or packages brought to me by inmates who were doing labor at the camp. The intermediary was always different. In order to be recognized, I wore a silk string around my throat, for a necklace. In turn, I had to pass on the letter or the package to a man carrying the same sign. Often I had to seek him in the washroom or on the road where the men were working.

In the beginning I did not know much of the nature of the enterprise in which I was participating. But I knew that I was doing something useful. That was enough to give me the strength. I was no longer prey to crises of depression. I even forced myself to eat enough to be able to fight on. To eat and not let oneself become enfeebled — that, too, was a way to resist.

We lived to resist and we resisted to live.

*   *   *   *

Dr. Mitrovna, the Russian surgeon in our hospital, was the first Russian woman I had ever met. I knew women from many countries, and I was anxious to learn about the women from the Soviet Union.

She was a powerful, buxom, dark-haired woman with expressive brown eyes that seemed to look right through you. She was a real doctor who was very fond of her patients and fought for them. When Dr. Mengerle selected a very sick woman for transfer to a "central hospital," she resisted tooth and nail, and firmly declared, "No, she is well. We will discharge her in three days." It was surprising that Mengerle gave in.

She created an atmosphere of respect. Yet she was the most natural and warmhearted person I have ever known. No one had as great a capacity for work as this fifty-year-old woman. When she saw that I was white from fatigue and still labored on, she would say, "You could be a good Russian." That was the greatest praise she could offer.

When the Russians bombed the S.S. kitchens in Birkenau, many inmates were hurt. I watched her carefully, would she show favoritism toward her compatriots? She treated everyone impartially and repeated the same caressing words to everyone: *"Charashov, charashov"* (There, there).

On Christmas eve, she joined the festivities and danced with the nurses. Although she had no voice, she sang like a child,

158

without self-consciousness. She told us that at home she had been fond of holidays because the food was always better. At the same time, we could see that she respected the religious spirit of her neighbors in the camp.

"We should remember this Christmas eve in captivity," she told us. "People from all the nations of Europe are together and hoping for the same thing . . . . freedom."

Later I met other Russian women: aggressive ones; and also kind, gentle souls. From them I realized that Communism is like a religion to the Russian people. Perhaps their faith helped them to endure the difficulties of life in Auschwitz-Birkenau better than the other inmates.

Each time a patient had to be sent to the hospital at Camp F, Dr. Mitrovna decided who should be the stretcher bearers. The first time I left the camp for this reason and the gates closed behind me, I began to cry. We were being followed by our guards, but the hated barbed wires were not so close. There was a little more space, and we could breathe freely. For these reasons it was worth anything to me to be chosen for this task.

It took fifteen minutes for the five of us to carry the sick women to the surgical barrack. There I saw another drama. The doctors saved many of the inmates through their surgery, and the Germans sent the patients straight to the gas chamber.

But the doctors played their roles with a calm dignity. I gazed about me in the operating room. The sight of the instruments and of the figures in white, and the smell of the ether reminded me of my husband and of our hospital in Cluj. I was lost in memories when suddenly someone whispered in my ear. "Don't move! No questions! Contact Jacques, French stubendienst, in hospital Barrack 30."

I was surprised. How did they know that I belonged to the Underground? Then I realized — the silk necklace.

I had an order and I must carry it out. But how? I was in a strange hospital camp for men, and I was a woman.

Suddenly a nurse announced that Dr. Mengerle was nearby.

The doctors tried to overcome their fright. There was a hubbub of excited voices.

"Hide the rubber gloves at once!"

"Open the door! He will smell the ether!"

I understood only too well. The good people had brought instruments and anaesthetics with their food rations. Now they had to hide everything if they did not want to be punished or even killed for being merciful.

Still the operation had to begin. The unfortunate woman on the table cried out in pain. It seemed as if she would have to be operated on without an anaesthetic.

"Those German beasts," I cursed. "I must reach Barrack 30!"

I started to leave when I saw blankets on the stretcher. Sick people wrapped in blankets were not a rare sight in the hospital camp. That was my solution.

I wrapped myself in one and ran out. Finally I found Jacques, the French male nurse, in Barrack 30. I told him that I had been ordered to go to him. He climbed to the top koia and took a small package from under a sick man's head.

"Give this to the glazier in your camp!" he commanded.

When I returned to the surgery barrack, my comrades were no longer there. The stretcher was gone. I ran to the camp entrance. The Russian doctor was arguing with the German. We had been in the men's camp for too long. And, I was absent.

When the Russian woman saw me coming with the blankets over my head, she understood. But she continued her dispute with the guard. "I told you that someone had taken away our blankets, and I sent this prisoner to bring them back. What is it that you cannot understand about it?" she argued.

She could only speak a little German; yet, perhaps, that saved us. A few Russian words, a few German words. Somehow the matter was settled. As we were hurrying back, I wondered when Mitrovna would ask for an explanation of where I had been. She asked nothing.

160

When we arrived at the camp I learned that the glazier had left! But the next day Jacques sent someone else, and I finally got rid of the parcel of explosive that had complicated my life so.

I wondered what Dr. Mitrovna really thought. She could have told the guard that I had left the group without permission, and wash her hands of the whole affair. Instead, she had waited for me. Observing that the blankets were missing from the stretcher, she had found a clever excuse, and saved me. She was, indeed, a good comrade.

I remember that I often saw the same worker who came to me with packages, in deep discussion with her. I can assume, therefore, that she, too, was a member of the camp resistance. This brilliant, silent woman could have known that I, too, belonged to the Underground. Perhaps that is why she did not protest when I left the surgery at Camp F, and why she saved me from the German guard.

We knew few others in the Underground because, in case of exposure, it was safer that way. Actually, Dr. Mitrovna may not have belonged. But there was something sterling in her character that made me believe she would have been with us — in everything.

*   *   *   *

At about three o'clock in the afternoon, on October 7, 1944, a terrific explosion rocked the camp. The internees gazed at each other in stupefaction. Where the crematory was located an immense column of flames was rising. The news spread like wildfire. The crematory oven had exploded!

Caught napping, the Germans completely lost their balance. They ran in every direction, shouting orders and counter-orders. Obviously, they feared a revolt. Under the threats of their guns they made us return to our barracks.

But what had actually happened? I took advantage of the

relative impunity which my infirmary blouse assured and left the hospital to sneak up to the kitchens. The latter were about ten yards from the camp entrance and looked out on the road to the crematories. It made an excellent observation post.

Several detachments of soldiers were already coming toward the camp, some in trucks, others on motorcycles. Then the infantry of the Wehrmacht arrived, followed by lorries with munitions. The soldiers surrounded the crematory and opened up with machine gun fire. I shuddered, why? A few scattered revolver shots replied. Was this a rebellion? A few more machine gun volleys and the Wehrmacht and S.S. stormed the place.

What had happened?

The resistance group of the Sonderkommando, the slaves of the gas chambers, had conceived a plan for blowing up the ovens. Through members of the Pasche group, they had procured a quantity of explosives, sufficient to carry out their project. But a number of things went wrong, and the explosion destroyed only one of the four buildings.

The revolt was organized by a young French Jew named David. Knowing that he was condemned to death anyway, since all members of the Sonderkommando were liquidated every three or four months, he decided to employ usefully what little time of life remained to him. It was he who had obtained the explosives and he who had hidden them. Then unforeseen events thwarted his plans.

The Germans advanced the date for the execution of the Sonderkommando. One day they gave them the order to be ready for transport and to leave the crematory building. The first group, about one hundred men, obeyed. But the second group protested. The attitude of these Sonderkommando, most of whom were robust, strapping fellows, became menacing. The few S.S. were so surprised that they prudently withdrew for orders and reinforcements. When they returned, one oven, which, in the meantime, had been crammed with explosives and

162

sprinkled with gasoline, blew up. The rebels did not have time to blow up the other three. However, the Sonderkommando of the fourth oven took advantage of the disorder, cut the barbed wire, and succeeded in slipping out of camp. Some of the men were stopped, but the rest managed to escape.

In the battle that ensued, the Sonderkommando resisted ferociously. They had nothing but sticks, stones, and a few revolvers to fight against trained killers armed with automatic weapons. Four hundred and thirty were captured alive, including David, their chief, who was fatally wounded.

The retaliation was horrible. The S.S. made the prisoners get down on hands and knees. Two or three S.S. shot each in the nape of the neck with devilish precision. Those who raised their heads to see if their turns were near received twenty-five lashes from the whip before being shot.

After this revolt, a number of reprisals followed in the camp Beatings became more frequent, as did mass selections. Dr. Mengerle, angry, personally used his revolver to slaughter several selectees who tried to elude him. His subordinates followed his example. Until the next rain the soil of the camp was thick with blood.

As for the several hundred Sonderkommandos who had not taken part in the rebellion, they were shot in groups in the nearby forest. In this way, Dr. Pasche, the French doctor in the sonderkommando and an active member of the camp underground, perished. It was he who had furnished us with the data on the activity of the Sonderkommando. L. who saw him shortly before his death, told us with what exemplary courage he spoke of his approaching death.

Were we discouraged that the explosion should have been a failure? We were chagrined, of course; but that it could take place at all was proof that times were changing even in Auschwitz-Birkenau.

CHAPTER XXI

"Paris Is Liberated"

During the workers' rest period on August 26, 1944, a French internee appeared in the infirmary. I had seen him before, a little dark-eyed, thin-faced man with the bitter expression typical of us in Birkenau. He was the same man and yet not the same; I could not understand his sly grin, the twinkle in his eyes, the satisfaction on his face, his assurance, the way he stretched out his hand for treatment. I gazed at him piercingly. "What can this mean?" I wondered. "Perhaps my eyes are deceiving me, but he looks as if he has grown taller."

His strange happiness made me feel uneasy. The inmates were always being overcome with desperation and here was one who seemed ready to burst for joy.

It occurred to me, "I must be careful. Poor fellow, there is something wrong with him." Such cases were not rare. I looked impatiently toward the door. He observed my reaction and bent his head to me. "Paris is liberated," he whispered.

I stood motionless. I was so startled I could not speak. I stared at him and forgot the treatment.

I was overcome, and at once understood the strange happiness in the little Frenchman. I still could not believe it. For a moment I thought, "Perhaps he really is mad." Then I wanted to shout, to do something. I roared with hysterical laughter.

Whenever I heard that the Allies had suffered reverses, I had to make a great effort to conceal my sorrow and invent good

164

news. For the morale of the internees had to be maintained. How happy I was when I could finally whisper to one patient after another that the Allies had really occupied Paris.

"Paris is liberated!"

The first patient to whom I told this news was a woman with swollen feet. She listened, opened her eyes wide with wonder, and drew her infected feet from the stool. Without a word, she began to cry. We cried together. The news was too wonderful to be accepted other than with simple joy.

How quickly the word spread! In the washrooms and in the latrines, the inmates hugged and kissed one another. In the hospital, the bedridden ones raised themselves on their elbows and beamed and nodded.

Everyone added something to the original report. By evening, our imaginations had all Europe liberated by the "Tommies." All English-speaking soldiers were "Tommies" to us.

The French prisoners could not be spoken to for days. They walked with their heads in the clouds. On the secret radio, the Pasche group dared to listen to General de Gaulle's speech from Paris. We learned of the heroism of the Parisians who had erected barricades and prevented the Germans from destroying the beauties of this lovely heart of France.

We felt that our cup was overflowing, and during the roll-call we gave our comrades signs through the corners of our eyes. Everybody knew what the wink meant.

The German reaction came immediately. The soup was, if possible, worse than before. A Pole and three Frenchmen were hanged for disseminating "false news." They shot the "Czar," a Russian engineer who, despite his nickname, was a rabid Communist. Nameless other thousands were again exterminated in the gas chamber this eve of the great Allied victory.

After the liberation of the "City of Light," our imaginations reeled, and we made bewildering plans. At night we discussed how we should receive the Allies. Airplanes would suddenly appear over Auschwitz, and parachutists would drop. On the

165

great day we would look up at the sky and see American, British, and Russian parachutes instead of the crematory cinders. Our German oppressors would be stricken with terror! They would kneel before us and implore mercy.

We would greet our liberators with kisses. It had not occurred to us that we were dirty and ragged, and our kisses would certainly be far from desirable. In any case, we decided that we would make beautiful dresses from the parachute silk.

*   *   *   *

"All internees who have relatives in America will be exchanged for German prisoners of war. These internees must give the names and addresses of their American relatives and all personal data about themselves, including name, former address, date of birth, etc." This order brought new excitement to the inmates of the camp. Every prisoner racked her brain day and night trying to remember the name of some distant relative in America. A few even wept because they could not recall the name of a cousin; others because they had not kept in contact with their overseas relatives.

Many internees had the necessary names, and a long list was compiled. Numbers of us already planned to spend Christmas in America, if all went well. We had been tricked so many times by the Germans, and still we were ready to believe again. I thought back to the incident of the deadly postcards. But even the blocovas did not know what to believe this time.

Some weeks later, the "Americans," as we were already calling them, were assembled by the Germans. They were given new clothing and were taken to the railroad station. They waited a long time before the cattle cars were ready, but they got in cheerfully.

The news spread throughout the entire camp: "The 'Americans' are starting out!" We rushed to the far end of the camp to see them leave.

166

The Germans had even given the "Americans" coats. The travelers waved with their hands to show us that some of them even had gloves. Others lifted their feet to show us their shoes. It was all the more surprising, because the Germans did not drive us away from the station.

"How wonderful it must be to be one of those 'Americans,'" we sighed as we plodded back to the barracks. We were downcast and jealous. For the first time we did not swarm about the Stubendienst at the distribution of the food. The blocova was amazed to see the internees sitting quietly, thoughtfully eating their slop while they dreamed of the great opportunity they had missed.

About two weeks later, a member of the Pasche group told me about the "Americans." They were taken to another camp in the neighborhood. "To wait until everything is ready for the final departure," they were told.

Evidently something was wrong. For the whole situation suddenly changed. The dresses and shoes that had been given to the "Americans" were quietly returned to the camp's warehouses. The poor "Americans" had been exterminated.

*　　　*　　　*　　　*

A few days after the departure of the "Americans," I learned that an American citizen was among the deportees in Barrack 28. I heard about him from a worker who usually labored in our camp.

The American was Dr. Albert Wenger, lawyer and economics expert. He had been in Vienna when Hitler declared war. The Swiss Consulate tried to have him returned to the United States through Switzerland. But it was not allowed, because the unfortunate Wenger had committed the grave "crime" of sheltering a Jewess. He was arrested and sent to Auschwitz-Birkenau.

I tried to get in touch with him, as I did with other American citizens here, but I was unsuccessful.

After liberation, I saw the official declaration he had made to the representatives of the liberating armies. I include part of it to show the American people how their citizens were treated in Germany:

"After Hitler had declared war on the United States, I had to go to the Commissariat twice a week as an enemy alien. The Swiss Consulate made a proposition to exchange me and send me back to the United States; despite that, I was arrested on February 24, 1943, by the Gestapo because I sheltered a Jewess without declaring her. I was taken, as a deportee, to the concentration camp at Auschwitz. I arrived there on March 6, dirty and starving, after spending much time in various police camps and prisons.

"The weather was cold and damp, and as a welcome, I was put in an alley between two barracks, nude, after a cold shower. Following that, I was dressed in a thin summer suit and sent into a quarantine barrack. Here the men were molested and beaten on every occasion. We did not know when access to the latrines was free, and when we were caught there, we were beaten with a rubber truncheon . . . .

"We had to sleep — four of us — in a bed seventy-five centimeters large. Our lives were nothing but torture, not only during the day but even at night. Fortunately, I fell ill on March 23. I caught a sore throat and pneumonia, and on the 24th, I was admitted to the building for the sick people: Barrack No. 28.

"After I had recovered, I worked first as a male nurse and barrack "Schreiber" (scribe), and finally as a barrack overseer. The food was composed, to a large degree, of water, rutabagas, and rotten potatoes. Under such a regime, most of the deportees became feeble and grew thin right under our eyes, and changed into would-be Musulmans. In this condition, they were admitted into the infirmary for any sickness; for example, diarrhea, pneumonia, etc.

"The camp doctor, Dr. Endress, came every three weeks to choose the most feeble among the Musulmans. The next day the open trucks arrived, and on them these unfortunates, dressed often in only a shirt, were thrown like animals at the slaughterhouse. They were

168

taken to Birkenau to be killed in the gas chamber; following that, they were burned in the crematory ovens.

"I affirm this since I have been convinced by the following considerations: 1) Their effects were sent back from Birkenau the next day to be disinfected. On the ordinary transports, when the departees were left alive, the clothing was never returned. In this way, the camp salvaged the underwear and clothing that had been given to the deportees. 2) As to the fate of these people, I was convinced on account of the lists I have seen at the principal offices. I learned that the fifth and the sixth, and often even on the third day, these names and numbers (the selectionees) were already inscribed on the lists as "dead." Generally, the assassination by gas of the feeble and undesirable deportees was a secret to nobody, because many deportees worked at the crematory and were not silent, but spoke about it from time to time with other deportees. Even the camp commander, the "Hauptsturmfuehrer" Hessler, in order to end the panic which reigned among the deportees, made a speech in Barrack No. 28 of the central camp of Auschwitz, in which he wanted to pacify the deported Jews by telling them that there would be no more gassings. That happened in the month of January, 1945, and confirmed the veracity of my affirmations.

"Up to April, 1943, it made no difference who was killed by the gas. After that date, only the Jews and the Gypsies were so killed. The non-Jewish undesirables were slaughtered in Barrack No. 11 or killed by an injection of phenol in the heart. These injections of phenol were executed, at the beginning, by the Oberscharfuehrer Klaehr, then by the Oberscharfuehrer Scheipe, the Unterscharfuehrer Hantel, the Unterscharfuehrer Nidowitzky (also called Napoleon), and by two inmates, Rausnik and Stessel, both of whom left with a transport.

"Among the deportees who were gassed were also the "protected deportee" (Schutzhaeftling) Joseph Iratz, of Vienna. (Probably by error, for the 'protected deportees' were not supposed to be gassed, according to the rules.)

"From my transport (two hundred fifty 'protected deportees' in all), four were gassed. In January, 1944, the United States citizen, Herbert Kohn, who was very feeble, was gassed. I succeeded in saving him from a few previous selections, but then he changed his barrack and could not avoid his fate. Kohn·was arrested by the Gestapo in France during a raid and was sent to Auschwitz as a Jew. Another American citizen, Myers, from New York, was gassed. He was from another barrack. I could enumerate many more similar cases, but, unfortunately, I cannot remember the names.

"In Autumn, 1943, the German protected inmate,' Willi Kritsch, 28 years old, an architect, was beaten with a stick by Unterscharfuehrer Nidowitzky in one of his fits of sadism until Kritsch fell to the ground. As Kritsch was still living, Nidowitzky ordered that he be taken to the operation room where he (Nidowitzky) injected him with phenol. The cause of death was stated to be 'weakness of the heart!'

"Every two or three months mass shootings took place against the black wall of Barrack No. 11. During these executions the barrack was closed and only the personnel of the hospital had the right to pass in front of it. I myself saw, at the end of 1943, or the beginning of 1944, how the male nurses threw the unclothed corpses on a large truck. These were the bodies of men and young women and healthy people. When the first truck was loaded, a second came, and the game was continued thusly: a torrent of blood ran through Barracks Nos. 10 and 11. The inmates of the disinfecting barrack and of the sick-people's building, sprinkled the blood with their sand and ashes.

"In October, 1944, the commercial councilor from Vienna, Berthold Storfer, was called to Barrack No. 11, and he never returned. A few days later I learned about his fate from the principal employee of the office. This one showed me the indication 'death,' on Storfer's personal card. In the same way Dr. Samuel of Cologne perished. Both of them were killed probably because they saw and learned too much. In November, 1943, Dr. Ritter von Burse accused Joseph Rittner, the locomotive driver from Austria, Dr. Arwin Valentin from Berlin, the surgeon, and Dr. Masur, the Berlin veterinarian, and me, of being against the German Reich and of having called the S.S. a

170

band of assassins and Hitler and Himmler, assassins of human masses.

"We were also supposed to have affirmed that Germany was very close to losing the war. We must thank the lawyer, Wolkinsky, that we were not shot. He had presented Burse as an adventurer and weakened the accusation. In order to make me confess, the S.S. Unterscharfuehrer Laehmann beat me.

"Shortly before our liberation by the Red Army, the new S.S. Hauptsturmfuehrer Krause beat without any reason two deportees who worked in the kitchen. One of them was the Dutch doctor, Ackermann. On January 25, 1945, the S.S. police tried again to make us go out of the camp in order to exterminate us. Only the rapid advance of the victorious Red Army allowed us to keep our lives."

CHAPTER XXII

Scientific Experiments

While I was working at the hospitals in Camp F. K. L. and Camp E., I had to take care of many human guinea pigs, the victims of the "scientific" experiments carried out at Auschwitz-Birkenau. The German doctors had hundreds and thousands of slaves at their disposal. Since they were free to do whatever they wished, they decided to experiment with these people. It was a rich windfall which decent men and women would have scorned, but which the Nazi medical contingent gloried in.

Not only did they make experiments, but they compelled many of the deportee doctors, too, to labor under the supervision of the S.S. physicians. Horrible as these experiments were, the men who had to conduct them might have been able to excuse themselves could they have believed that they were at least serving science and that the sufferings of these unfortunate guinea pigs might, in the end, spare others from suffering.

But there was no scientific benefit. Human beings were sacrificed by the hundreds of thousands, and that was all. So the shackled deportee doctors, almost all of whom finally ended in the crematory ovens, sabotaged the "experiments" as far as they could. Besides, such disorder and lack of method was evident in these "scientific experiments" that they were cruel games rather than serious quests for truth. Everyone has heard of heartless children who amuse themselves by tearing off the legs and wings of insects. Here there was one difference: the insects were human beings.

One of the most common experiments, and also one of the most useless, was the inoculation of a group of inmates with a disease germ. For, in the interim, the German doctors usually lost their interest in the project. As for the guinea pigs? When they were lucky, they were sent to the hospital; when they were not, they went to the gas chamber. Only in exceptional instances were they put under observation.

Often, the experiments were absolutely absurd. A German doctor conceived the idea of studying how long a human being could exist on nothing but salt water. Another submerged his human guinea pigs in ice water and claimed he could observe the effect of the bath on internal temperatures. After undergoing such experiments, the inmates needed no hospital, but were ready for the gas chamber. One day several nurses entered the infirmary and asked, "Who cannot sleep?" About twenty inmates accepted a dose of an unknown white powder, which might have had a morphine base. The next day ten were dead. The same experiments were conducted among the older women, and seventy more died the same night.

When the Germans sought new treatments for the wounds caused by American phosphorous bombs, they burned fifty Russians on the back with phosphorous. These "controls" received no medication. The men who survived were exterminated.

One of the favorite experiments was conducted on newly arrived women whose menstruation was still normal. During their periods, they were told roughly, "You will be shot in two days." The Germans wanted to know what effect such news would have on the menstrual flow. A professor of histology in Berlin even published an article in a German scientific periodical on his observation on hemorrhages provoked in women by such bad news.

Dr. Mengerle, the chief physician, had two favorite studies:

173

twins and dwarfs. From the first selections, the twins of each convoy were set apart, if possible with their mothers. Then they were sent to Camp F. K. L. No matter what their age or sex, twins interested Mengerle deeply. They were favored and even allowed to keep their clothing and their hair. He went so far in his solicitude for twins that when they were exterminating the Czech Camp, he gave orders to spare a dozen sets of twins.

Upon arrival, twins were photographed from every possible angle. Then the experiments began, but these were disconcertingly juvenile in character. For example, one twin would be inoculated with certain chemical substances, and the doctor was to watch for the reaction, if he did not happen to forget about it. But even when the doctor followed through, there was no gain for science for the simple reason that the product injected offered no particular interest. Once they used a preparation that was supposed to cause a change in the pigmentation of the hair. Many days were lost in pondering over the hair and examining it under a microscope. The results showed nothing sensational, and the experiments were allowed to lapse.

Dwarfs were Dr. Mengerle's greatest passion. He collected them zealously. The day he discovered a family of five dwarfs in a transport he was beside himself with joy. But his was the mania of a collector, not of a savant. His experiments and observations were carried out in an abnormal fashion. When he made transfusions, he purposely used incorrect blood types. Of course complications followed. But Mengerle had no one to account to but himself. He did whatever pleased him and conducted his experiments like a mad amateur.

One experimental station which was installed some distance from the camp appeared to have a more scientific character. But only at first glance. There one could see that the "work" was only a criminal debauchery of human material and a total lack of scruples on the part of the inquirers. The experiments were theoretically intended to gather information for the Wehrmacht. Most of the time, they consisted of tests of human endurance, resistance to cold or to heat, or to high altitudes. Hundreds of internees died in the course of these experiments in the Auschwitz station, as well as in other camps. At the price of the lives of thousands of victims, German science finally concluded that a human being can subsist in ice water, at a predetermined temperature, for just so many hours. It had also been established with precision (!) how long it took for death to come after scaldings at different degrees of temperature.

I have mentioned experiments to determine the resistance of the human organism to hunger. Musulmans, especially the most emaciated specimens, were forced to drink unbelievable quantites of soup. These cramming experiments were often fatal. I heard of a few cases where the deportees, suffering horribly from hunger, volunteered for this forced feeding. The son of Prime Minister M., was so famished that he offered himself as a guinea pig for malaria experiments. The subjects of this experiment received double bread rations for a few days.

Experiments were also made in diagnostics. Interesting cases were taken from the hospital and simply killed so that they could be dissected for the purpose of an autopsy! When several cases suffered from the same ailment, they might be given different treatments and, after a certain phase, be killed, so that conclusions might be drawn from the experiments. Most of the time a patient was killed, and no one dreamed of examining his body — there were too many dead in Auschwitz.

The German Bayer Company sent medicines in vials with no labels to indicate their contents. People suffering from tuberculosis were injected with this product. They were not sent to the gas chamber. Their overseers waited for them to die, and death came quickly. After that, parts of the lungs were taken to a laboratory chosen by Bayer.

Once the Bayer Company bought one hundred and fifty women from the camp administration and experimented on them with unknown medicaments, perhaps for hormone tests.

The Weigel Institute of Cracow sent vaccines to the camp.

These, too, had to be experimented on and "improved." The victims were chosen from French political prisoners, especially members of the French underground whom the Germans wanted to be rid of.

About two thousand organic preparations had to be dispatched to the University of Innsbruck. According to instructions, these preparations had to be made from absolutely healthy bodies, which had been gassed, hanged, or shot, *while in good health!*

One day a large number of women, mostly Polish, were used for vivisection experiments: grafting of the bones and muscles, and various others. German surgeons arrived from Berlin to make the experiments and watch the result. The vivisections were carried out under terrible conditions. The victim was bound to the operating table in a primitive barrack, and the operation was made *without aseptic care.* Even after the operations, the human guinea pigs suffered terribly. They were given nothing to alleviate their sufferings.

To enrich their racial science, the Germans regularly extracted blood. Apart from the scientific interest, the blood of the internees was used for transfusions to German wounded. Five hundred cc. of blood were taken from each "voluntary" donor and sent immediately to the army. To save the lives of the Wehrmacht soldiers, the Germans forgot that Jewish blood was "of inferior quality."

I have already mentioned the "injections in the heart," as the inmates called the intracardiac injections of phenol. Sometimes, these intracardiac injections were made with benzine or petroleum. This method was used in the hospitals to kill the sick or the feeble and the "superfluous."

I spoke to a Polish doctor who was forced to give these injections to his fellow inmates for two days.

"When the S.S. doctor called me to the hospital," he told me, "I did not know what it was all about. He ordered me to inject the patients in the cardiac cavity. He told me that I should

176

inject the liquid as soon as I had proof that the needle was in the cardiac cavity."

The Polish doctor followed orders, and the patients then fell dead on the floor.

In another mad experiment they laid hundreds of sick out in the blazing sun. The Germans wanted to know how long it would take a sick person to die under the sun without water.

Twenty miles from our camp was an experimental station which specialized in artificial insemination. To this station were sent the most endowed of the doctor inmates and the most beautiful of the women. The Germans attached great importance to these experiments. Unfortunately, I could not see the work that went on there, for this station was the most jealously guarded of all. Some data, however, I did obtain.

The Germans practiced artificial insemination on a number of women, but the investigations offered no results. I knew women who had been subjected to artificial insemination and had happened to survive, but they were ashamed to admit the experiments.

Another group was injected with the sex hormones. It had not been possible to determine the nature of the substance injected or the results the Germans obtained. After these injections, many women had abscesses which were lanced in Barrack 10.

But I am well informed on the sterilization experiments. These took place in Auschwitz-Birkenau under the direction of a Polish doctor who was executed by the Germans a few days before the camp was evacuated.

These experiments attempted to compare the results of the surgical methods and X-ray treatments. At the hospital, we saw numerous sick women who had come from this experimental station. They showed serious burns caused by the clumsy application of these rays. Through them and the deportee doctors we learned about the experiments. The subject was placed under X-ray radiation, which was made more and more intense. From time to time the treatment was interrupted in order to see if the subject could still copulate. All this took place under the vigilant eyes of the S.S. in Barrack 21. When the physician verified that the X-rays had definitely destroyed the genital faculties, this subject was dispatched to the gas chamber. Occasionally, when the irradiation took too long to produce the desired effect, the victim was castrated surgically.

In August, 1944, the Germans sterilized about one thousand boys between the ages of thirteen and sixteen. Their names and the dates of sterilization were registered. After some weeks the boys were brought to Barrack 21. In the laboratory they were questioned about the result of the first "treatment," their desires, nocturnal pollutions, loss of memory, etc.

Then the Germans forced them to masturbate. They provoked the erection by massaging the prostate glands. When this work tired the "masseur," the German "scientists" used a metal instrument, which caused the patient great pain.

The sperm was examined by a bacteriologist who determined the vitality of the spermatozoa. In 1944, the Germans sent a phosphorescent microscope to the camp. This enabled them to see the difference between the living and the dead spermatozoa.

Sometimes the Germans made incomplete castrations: a quarter or a half of the testicle was removed. Sometimes the whole testicle was sent to Breslau in a tube sterilized with formalin (10 per cent) for an histopathological study of the tissues. These operations were made with intrarachidian injections of novocaine. The boys were separated from the others in Barrack 21 and were closely watched. When the experiments were finished, the reward was, as usual, the gas chamber.

I remember one case of a Polish boy named Gruenwald, who was about twenty years old. Professor Klauber ordered treatment with X-rays. After two months the X-rays had not produced the desired effect. So the boy was taken to Barrack 21 for a complete castration. But the X-rays had been given in such doses that he had been seriously burned. Cancer followed and the boy suffered terribly. In January, 1945, he was still alive in the hospital at Birkenau.

These methods were also applied to the women. Sometimes the Germans used short-wave rays which caused unbearable pains in the lower part of the abdomen. Then the belly of the sick woman was *opened* to observe the lesions. The surgeons usually removed the uterus and the ovaries.

Professor Schuman and Dr. Wiurd made many such experiments on young girls about sixteen or seventeen years old. Of the fifty girls used for this experiment, only two survived, Bella Schimski and Dora Buyenna, both from Salonika. They told us that they had been put under short-wave rays, one plate placed on the abdomen and the other on the back. The electricity was directed toward the ovaries. The dose was so great that the subjects were gravely burned. After two months of observation, the girls had to suffer a "control" operation.

A group of young women, mostly Dutch, were subjected to a series of experiments for which only the author, Klauberg, German gynecologist of Kattowitz, could have known the reason. With the aid of an electrical apparatus, a thick whitish liquid was infused into the genital organs of these women. It caused a terrible burning sensation. This infusion, repeated every four weeks, was each time followed by a radioscopy.

These same women were simultaneously subjected to another series of experiments by another doctor. This time it was an injection in the chest. The physician injected five cc. of a serum, whose nature I do not know, at the rate of from two to nine injections each session. The reaction came in the form of a painful swelling the size of a fist. Certain women received more than a hundred of these innoculations. Some were also injected in the gums. After a number of such experiments the women were declared useless and sent away.

Once we asked an Aryan German inmate, a former social worker, for the basic reason for the sterilization and castration. Before his captivity he had been active in German politics and had known many eminent people. He told us that the Germans had a geopolitical reason for these experiments. If they could sterilize all non-German people still alive after their victorious war, there would be no danger of new generations of "inferior" peoples. At the same time, the living populations would be able to serve as laborers for about thirty years. After that time, the German surplus population would need all the space in these countries, and the "inferiors" would perish without descendants.

When I think of these experiments, I cannot help but recall the drama of the little French woman, Georgette, who died at the hospital on Christmas day, 1944. She had been used as a guinea pig in sterilization experiments, and when she returned to the hospital she was no longer a female.

Georgette had a Polish fianceé, who was to visit her on that day. But she was resolved never to see him again. Rather than admit her degradation, she chose to pass for dead.

The lover came, but Georgette hid under the blanket on the third tier of the koia as immobile as though dead. Because the sick woman desired it, we had told him the day before that she now was dead. But he had not come to see Georgette. He went to the bed of another young girl, from Cracow, to whom he had brought his gifts.

From under her cover, Georgette saw everything. With her last remaining strength she raised herself and threw herself from the top of the koia. The fall was fatal.

CHAPTER XXIII

Love in the Shadow of the Crematory

Nature dictates that wherever men and women are together there shall also be love. Even in the shadow of the crematory the emotions could not be entirely suppressed. Love, or what passed for it in the degraded atmosphere of the death camp, was but a distortion of what it is for normal people, for society in Birkenau was but a distortion of a normal human society.

The supermen in charge of our destinies sought to extinguish every desire in the inmates. Camp gossip had it that certain powders were mixed into our food to reduce or destroy sexual appetite. So that the S.S. might not become overly excited by the presence of many young and beautiful internees whom they saw naked and in every degree of exposure, there were brothels supplying German prostitutes for their use. Despite the Nazi theories on racial pollution, we heard that a number of attractive internees were drafted for these brothels. Similar privileges were available to inmates in the men's camps. Admission for the inmates was, naturally, to be regarded as an exceptional favor.

Furthermore, rules and artificial procedures counted for nothing. The constant nervous tension under which we lived did little to depress our desires. On the contrary, the mental anguish seemed to provide a peculiar stimulus.

The relations among the internees of both sexes were characterized by the absence of social conventions. Everyone addressed everyone else in the familiar "thou," and by the first

181

name. Such familiarity did not imply solidarity, nor was it always entirely free from vulgarity.

The only men we met besides the S.S. guards and the Wehrmacht troops were male internees who did road repairs, ditch-digging, and similar tasks in our camp. As a rule the only time that we mixed was during lunch, either in the washroom or in the latrines where many of the men ate their food. They were usually surrounded by women of all ages and shapes who clamored piteously for crumbs.

The women stood around them in circles, three or four deep, their hands stretched forth like beggars. Pretty girls sang the latest songs to attract attention. Sometimes the men relented and gave away parts of their lunch. Only then could a woman enjoy a potato, that most luscious of camp luxuries which was ordinarily reserved only for the kitchen workers and the blocovas.

Yet it was rarely pity that made the men share their not-too-abundant food. For food was the coin that paid for sexual privileges.

It would be heartless to condemn women who had to sink so low for a half crust of bread. The responsibility for the degradation of the internees rested with the camp administration.

Be that as it may, prostitution with all its lamentable consequences: venereal diseases, pimps, etc., was an ordinary phenomenon at Birkenau. Many of the objects stolen in "Canada" were destined for the women of those men who were smartest in these exchanges.

However, all love here was not sordid. There were instances of sincere and touching affection and companionship. But even where tenderness was absent, a woman with a lover enjoyed real distinction, for there were very few men in the camp.

Most of the younger women achieved flirtations. The blocovas, who had private corners in the barracks, were at an advantage which they did not hesitate to use. Cronies of the blocova acted as sentinels while the chief entertained her guest.

182

Of course, these rendezvous were strictly *verboten*. When an S.S. approached the block, the watchers sounded the alert. It often happened that a rendezvous was disturbed three or four times, but the couples were not easily discouraged.

Occasionally the blocova might, for a reasonable consideration, lease her quarters to a friend. The compensation was high, for the risk was great. If caught receiving a man, or even facilitating such a meeting, the blocova faced severe punishments. Her hair would be shaved again, she would be beaten unmercifully, and, worst of all, she would be demoted from her exalted rank.

Standards of beauty vary. In Birkenau, a world apart, the woman with the fullest figure and the most opulent charms was considered the ultimate in female pulchritude. The male inmates, themselves reduced to living skeletons, were repelled by bony bodies and hollow cheeks. Those women — few enough — who miraculously retained some flesh were envied by others who, a year earlier, would have endured tortuous diets to reduce their weight.

As in all prisons, Birkenau had its perverts. Among the women there were three categories. Those who were lesbians by instinct formed the least interesting group. More troublesome was the second classification, which included women who, because of the abnormal conditions, suffered changes in their sexual viewpoint. Often they yielded under the pressure of necessity.

We had a Polish woman, about forty, who had once been a professor of physics. Her husband had been killed by the Germans and her children shipped off to some dread place, perhaps to death. One of the prisoners, a functionary, paid particular court to this lovely, delicate, and intelligent woman. The professor knew that if she responded she would at least be spared from hunger. She must have fought a great battle against the temptation, but in the end, she surrendered. Six weeks later she was referring to her "friend" with much enthusiasm. In

183

another two months she declared that she could not live without her consort.

In the third category were those who, unlike my Polish acquaintance, discovered their lesbian predilections through an association with corruption. This was encouraged by the "dance soireés" that were sometimes organized in this Dantesque world of Birkenau. During the long winter nights of 1944, when the Germans were more preoccupied with the advancing Russians than with us, the inmates gave "parties" that parodied gruesomely the mundane affairs they had known in the old life. They gathered around a charcoal bin to sing and dance. A guitar and a harmonica from the camp orchestra helped these parties to continue until daybreak.

The heads of our barracks played a prominent role in these affairs. The lageraelteste, the "uncrowned queen of the camp," who was an inmate at Camp E where I now lived, was always present. She was a young, fragile thing, a German girl of about thirty. She managed to exist for ten years, knocking about from one camp to another.

During these orgies the couples who danced together gradually became attached to each other. Some of the women assumed male attire to lend an air of reality to the proceedings.

One of the chief initiators of these soireés was a Polish countess whose name I don't recall. When I first saw her, she was sitting in the doorway of our hospital. I looked at her in surprise. "What is that man doing in this place?" I wondered. For she looked exactly like a male. She wore a black velvet artist's jacket, the kind that was familiar in the Parisian art quarter, and a flowing black bow tie. Even her hair was cut short in mannish fashion. She really seemed to be a handsome man of about thirty. When I questioned a fellow inmate, I was told, "This 'man' is not a man — 'He' is a she!"

In her general behavior and mannerisms the countess acted like a man. Once when I had crawled up into the koias because I was on "Lice Control Duty," I felt a courteous hand assisting my descent. I was indeed surprised. But it was the countess! With this gallant gesture, she opened a siege of courtship. I actually had to run to escape her.

While the others cavorted about during the dances, I was often asleep in my bunk. On many an occasion, I was awakened by kisses and other amorous gestures. The countess! It got so that I feared to sleep during the dances. The others were amused by her ardent courtship, but I was not. They had expected the countess to seek a new attachment; her former "girl friend" had been removed in a transport.

I was sorry for this unhappy woman. German humor had placed her in our camp. When she had arrived she had been dressed in men's clothing, and the Germans had wanted to place her in the male camp. She argued desperately and tried to prove that she was a woman. They obliged her, for it was a three-ring circus for our captors to observe the antics of this "man-woman" amongst us. Of course, we dared not complain or protest. It amused the Germans.

The soireés always reminded me of the "Dance Macabre." When I thought of the common fate that waited these unfortunates, I could not repress a shiver of horror.

But perhaps my disgust was groundless under the circumstances. The horrible distractions provided a few hours of forgetfulness, and that in itself was worth almost anything in the camp. Besides these parties were better than many other things that took place there. The prisoners, men or women, were frequently abused by the German barrack leaders, among whom was a high percentage of homosexuals and other perverts.

I shall never forget the agony of one mother who told me that she was forced to undress her daughter and to look on while the girl was violated by dogs whom the Nazis had specially trained for this sport. That happened to other young girls. They were compelled to labor in the quarries for twelve or fourteen hours a day. When they dropped from exhaustion their guards'

185

favorite form of amusement was to urge the dogs to attack them. Who can forgive them all the crimes they committed?

The heads of the camp were noted for their aberrations. The Griese woman was bisexual. My friend, who was her maid, informed me that Irma Griese frequently had homosexual relationships with inmates and then ordered the victims to the crematory. One of her favorites was a blocova, who survived as Irma's slave a long time before the camp chief tired of her.

Such was the polluted atmosphere of Birkenau, a hell unto itself. Here the Nazis trampled on the most private of all rights. Here love became corrupt excitement for the slaves and sadistic entertainment for the overseers.

* * * *

I was afraid of Irma Griese. Once I offered my margarine ration as a bribe to keep from appearing before her. I made the proposal to Griese's dressmaker, who was called Madame Grete and had once owned a Viennese or a Budapest fashion salon.

Madame Grete was cross with me. "Why do you make difficulties?" she grunted. "It's your turn, and you know very well it's better to do as you're told." But at my continued pleading, she promised to hurry to the blocova's secretary to find someone else to help her deliver Irma Griese's wardrobe.

By morning I was looking forward to that rare coffee-spoon of margarine. I felt an overwhelming desire to eat it, but I did not want to show myself to Irma Griese.

I took the margarine to Madame Grete. She accepted it and stored it away. "Well, let's go," she said.

I trembled. "Couldn't you manage it?"

"No. You must come."

"But my margarine!"

"When we come back, you can have it. You can't take it with you, you know."

She took the neatly pressed clothes and laid them over my

186

outstretched arms, and we set out. We had a pass to leave the camp grounds for this purpose. A few minutes later we were outside the barrack where the blonde angel lived.

"You haven't come at the best time. The wild beast has gone insane," Irma Griese's servant whispered to us.

"Oh, my God! She'll beat me!" the dressmaker moaned.

"Surely not," I said, trying to show strength for both of us. "Day and night you sew for her, and she doesn't give you as much as a crust of bread."

"Don't you know?" they both asked in one voice. "Griese is a terrible sadist."

Screams and the sound of blows could be heard from behind Griese's closed door.

"She's at it again," the servant said.

We crept up to the wall of the wooden barrack. In a narrow opening between the slats, I could see only a part of the room inside. On the left someone was shrieking. By the cracks of a whip, someone was being beaten savagely. Griese was cursing in a hoarse voice. But all that was visible was the couch opposite the peep-hole. But in another moment the scene grew livelier.

Griese moved toward the sofa, dragging a naked woman by the hair. When she reached the divan, she sat down, but she did not release the woman's hair. She pulled the thick coil higher and higher, meanwhile bringing the handle of her whip down again and again across the woman's hips. The victim was forced to move closer and closer. Finally she knelt before her torturer.

"*Komm hier,*" Irma shouted toward a corner of the room which was out of my sight. And then again, "Come here. Are you coming or not?" And she raised the whip once more and fanatically belabored the woman at her feet.

Now, in the space that was visible to me appeared the figure of a male prisoner. It was the handsome Georgian. We knew him.

187

The man was unbelievably good looking. The Georgian race is said to produce the handsomest men, and this one was a perfect example. He was so tall that he nearly reached the ceiling of the barrack. Despite the terrible mistreatment and starvation, his robust chest was that of an athlete. His face had become lean with deprivation, but the features were all the more attractive. The story of this handsome Georgian had passed from mouth to mouth throughout the camp. He had been sent in to the women's lager to repair the road. Here he had met the delicate, madonna-like young Polish girl who now knelt, nude, under the blows of Irma Griese's whip.

The scene needed no explanation. We understood it. Irma had seen this splendid specimen of manhood, the handsome Georgian, and, like some eastern potentate, had picked him for herself. She had ordered him to her room. But when the proud young man, whose spirit had not been broken either by captivity or by Irma's terrifying reputation, had refused to yield to her wishes, Irma had tried to force him to become her slave by compelling him to look on while she tortured the girl he loved.

I know that this incident will appear preposterous and incredible to the American reader. But it is absolutely true, word for word. Other former prisoners at Auschwitz who were in contact with Irma Griese could testify to it in every particular.

Unfortunately (or thank God!), we could not stay to see the end of the scene, for a guard approached and we had to hurry away. So we waited to be summoned into the presence of the S.S. woman.

The door opened. First the man came out. I shall never forget his blazing dark eyes and his face filled with inexpressible hate. Then the Polish girl emerged. She was in a dreadful state. Red welts extended across her face and below the opening of her bosom. The sadistic S.S. had spared not even her face.

Irma commanded us to enter. She was flushed and was nervously buttoning her blouse. She uttered an hysterical laugh.

"All right. Let's try the things on," she ordered.

Madame began to hand her the dresses; I stood in the adjoining room holding the garments and waiting in terror for Griese to see me.

That fitting was a series of chilling scenes. I saw the beautiful beast naked. She wore only a chemise, but when she tried on one of the new undergarments she stripped altogether with no sign of embarrassment. We were not human beings before whom modesty might be necessary. The chemise she was trying was tailored to the figure, but it was too snug at the bosom, and with a single movement, Irma tore it open and tossed it into Madame's face. "Have this ready by tomorrow morning."

The dressmaker stuttered in deadly fear. "I c-can't have it ready by morning. I — I — have no light to sew by."

The naked demon rushed at the luckless modiste in a frenzy of rage, and struck her.

I scarcely dared to breathe. How could such animal fury dwell in so beautiful a body?

Minutes later, Irma proceeded with the fitting as if nothing had happened. When the fitting was over, she stretched wearily, yawned, and as if she were speaking to a pair of annoying servants, *"Heraus mit euch."* (Get out!).

We left this blonde in her lace slip. Her white skin brought out the pattern of the black lace. She was far from thin, but well formed; perhaps her breasts were a little too large. Also, she had heavy thick legs. It was the first time that I had seen her without the S.S. boots. I was happy to observe that she had an imperfection, she was so proud of her beauty.

I never saw the handsome Georgian again. The beautiful beast had him shot. The girl? From Irma's maid we found out about her, too. Griese had had her sent to the Auschwitz brothel.

189

CHAPTER XXIV

In the Death Car

During the long months, I did everything possible to find some trace of my husband. Each time a transport of men passed our camp, I hurried to the barbed wire with a pounding heart and scanned every deportee in a striped uniform. Perhaps he might be among them! In my dreams I often saw him working in the mines, standing in water up to his knees, or breaking rocks in the quarry. At least a hundred times I tried to send word to him. But I never knew whether my messages reached him or not. There was never a response. Imagine my joy then when at the end of six months, I learned through the underground that he was working in the camp at Buna, about twenty-five miles away. He was surgeon of the hospital, which was much better equipped than ours. From then on I had but one desire: to see him again. But how could I manage it?

One by one, after rejecting a thousand plans, I finally hit upon a solution. Our camp contained a block for insane people. The mad rulers of the camp dictated that, while normal people were sent to death, lunatics were kept alive. Most of these cases were "interesting," therefore priceless to the German savants.

Two or three times a week, various of our insane were taken to the experimental station at Buna, and then returned to Birkenau. For these transports, ambulances with red crosses were used: we called them "death" trucks because they also transported the victims to the gas chamber. Each time the

190

insane were accompanied by a few members of the hospital staff. Why could I not get to Buna as a nurse on one of these journeys?

Obviously, the attempt was filled with danger. First I had nothing to do with the barrack of the insane. They had their own nurses, most of whom the S.S. troops knew well. I risked a strong chance of being caught if I went in place of one of them. Besides, the transports did not always return to the barrack. Once the experiments were completed the human material was judged expendable and was taken to the gas chamber. Another risk was I could very easily be taken, not for a member of the hospital staff, but for one of the insane.

However, all that carried little weight. I would risk my life. Didn't I risk it anyway, every day?

I succeeded in getting a note to my husband indicating that he was to expect me at the hospital in Buna any day.

This time, a reply came. My husband counseled strongly against it and outlined all the perils. However, he added that if I did not want to change my mind, I should at least take every possible precaution. The chief doctor of the "insane barrack" could be useful in this respect.

After many unfruitful attempts, in the course of which I even tried to pass off myself as insane, I finally succeeded in getting a place in the famous death car.

Two nurses supervised seven or eight patients. The three S.S. guards who were convoying us locked the door and took their places beside the driver.

I shall never forget the mad journey. Excited by these changes, the insane people became agitated. They quarreled among themselves, fought with each other, and cried aloud. We tried to calm them, but without success. Sometimes they hugged and kissed us; other times they spit and overwhelmed us with insults.

The car traversed the city of Auschwitz. What I saw through the latticed glass gave the impression of an unreal world. Free

191

men were walking about in the streets, standing in queues, coming out of church, entering stores. Housewives, with baskets were shopping. Children were playing. No kapos, no clubs, no triangles on the clothing. It was not possible; I must have been dreaming.

The car continued to move. From time to time the S.S. guards peered through the window. The scene among the lunatics amused them prodigiously.

One of the insane, a real "Musulman," was masturbating continually. Two women were squeezing each other and making love on the floor of the car. Another, a Polish professor of mathematics, eloquently demonstrated with a great many gestures that the problem of the war could be reduced to a single equation with four unknowns: X, Y, Z, and V — Churchill, Roosevelt, Stalin, and Hitler. Meanwhile, the other insane were groaning or shouting. If I had had to remain in that car longer, I believe that it would have been my turn to lose my reason.

At last the ambulance stopped. We were at the hospital at Buna. Male nurses offered to help us take the sick down and carry them inside. We were passing the surgery section when a door opened, and I found myself face to face with my husband.

At the sight of me, he grew pale. I stood there speechless. How feeble and aged he had become. His features were drawn and his hair was gray. Beneath his white doctor's blouse I saw the striped prisoner's trousers. We did not greet each other, for we dared not let the guards understand what was going on.

The sick were led into an experimental room. There, under the surveillance of a German doctor, they were injected with a new product intended to produce a shock in the nervous system. The reactions were noted with much care.

While these experiments were going on, and our S.S. guards were eating and drinking in the German medical director's office, I was able to rejoin my husband. We found ourselves in an operating room, in the midst of the bright metal instruments and an atmosphere saturated with ether and chloroform. There was no comparison between our miserable place in Birkenau and this well-equipped establishment.

We were both embarrassed and did not know what to talk about. So many things had happened since our last meeting! How could we speak when all our thoughts were filled with mourning. On our lips we both had the names of our sons and of my parents, and of our many friends whom we had seen perish. But we uttered no names.

It was he who first found words of encouragement. In a few sober sentences, he told me about his life and of the satisfaction he derived from being able to ease the sufferings of so many internees. He was at the operating table from morning until night.

He tried to comfort me. He urged me not to let go of myself, for we had a task to fulfill in life. We must live to give proof of what we had seen and labor till the day of final justice. Lastly he begged me not to risk my life again by trying to see him at Buna. Besides, he added, these trips would probably be abolished soon.

It was indeed the last trip, as I was to learn a few days later.

The time passed so quickly! Already the insane were being taken towards the ambulance, completely exhausted from the experiments. I had to rejoin them.

Once I was in the truck, I saw my husband again. He was standing at the hospital door, his face wrinkled with anguish. This is the last picture I remember of him.

Later I learned what happened. A liberated French prisoner wrote me that Buna was evacuated and the internees driven away on a long march. Despite the explicit order of the Germans, my husband stooped over to help a French internee who had collapsed. He wanted to give the poor man an injection of a stimulant to keep him going. Immediately an S.S. guard opened fire and slaughtered both of them.

CHAPTER XXV

On the Threshold of the Unknown

On the morning of January 17, 1945, S.S. troops appeared at the hospital, assembled all the instruments of any value and loaded them on trucks.

At midnight other S.S. arrived and ordered us to bring the case records and the temperature charts to the "political bureau" immediately. In less than an hour, the documents were gathered in front of the bureau quarters. They were heaped upon the earth and made quite a mound of papers. An S.S. guard promptly set them on fire!

The Lageraelteste then summoned the personnel of the hospital and announced that the evacuation of the camp was imminent. Each of us was to gather her most indispensable effects and dress as warmly as possible. According to the news which she had received, we were to leave for the interior of Germany. However, she added gloomily, a change of plans was not unlikely. "They" might reach another decision with regard to our destinies. In any case, the sick were to remain behind.

One could not indulge in too many illusions. The Germans undoubtedly planned to exterminate our patients; unless they were overrun by the Russians, who could not be far away. As for us, two questions arose: would it be wiser to hide somewhere in the camp and wait for liberation? Or would it be better to leave with the rest and try to escape en route? Either course involved hazards. But the evacuation into the interior of Germany would mean death ultimately.

News of the proposed evacuation spread rapidly. A dense crowd pressed against the barbed wire which separated the men's camp from the women's. Husbands, lovers, friends called good-bye, wondering whether they would ever see each other again. Everyone was affected. Across the wires they cried out addresses of rendezvous where they might meet after the war. It was forbidden to have writing materials, so one had to memorize these precious bits of information!

The wildest rumors were rampant. Some affirmed that we would all be put to death on the road. Others declared that the Russians would be here in a few hours, and that we must wait for them there.

The hospital saw distressing scenes. The sick were in panic. Those who had any strength left at all leaped from their beds to reclaim their clothing. We distributed what we had, but we could not clothe more than a few. We followed orders and continued to take care of our patients. Besides, we were not all leaving together. Some, including the Italian woman doctor, Marinetti, had decided to stay on at all costs. Others did not feel strong enough to undertake another long trip.

But the sick people were not resigned. Those who had no clothing wrapped themselves in their blankets. None had shoes or stockings, and a real battle ensued over a few dozen pairs of wooden shoes which the Germans had given out — one pair for each twenty patients. These were intended for use on going to the latrines.

During that morning the Germans assembled us in the Lagerstrasse in columns of five. They made us wait an hour or two in spite of the bitter cold. Then they sent us back to the barracks.

In the afternoon the new camp commander arrived, escorted by a large entourage. At once a severe selection followed. All the sick, and even those who, not officially sick, appeared to be in poor physical condition, were sent into their barracks. Many wept. Others tried to slip into the groups that were leaving. But the S.S., always without pity, pursued them with sticks and with revolver shots.

As we were still waiting, I left the ranks to make the last hospital rounds. Order and discipline had disappeared. Most of the sick had left their beds, and were massing around the stove in the middle of the room. Some had invaded the blocova's room and, thanks to the hoard of food which they found, were making plazki in a frying pan.

I had to leave to take my place in the ranks again, but I gave a few injections to calm those whose sufferings were the most unbearable. I still hesitated. Should I stay? Should I leave? Someone called me. A comrade had come to warn me.

When I rejoined my group, I saw a long line beginning to march in the men's camp, on the other side of the barbed wire.

I glanced over the vast area of Birkenau. Before Camps F, D, C, and B-2 vast piles of paper were burning. The Germans were destroying every record of their crimes. They certainly did not want any trace to fall into the hands of the Russians.

A few minutes later, an inmate hurried up. "Get ready, quickly! We shall probably leave right after the men."

The gates opened, and a detachment of S.S. swarmed into our camp. We dispersed to get our bundles. Suddenly it occurred to me that we had no food. If we had to travel for several days, we would die from hunger.

"Hold on!" I cried to my companions who were running towards the barrack. "We cannot leave without bread. Let's smash in the warehouse door!"

I said this with such firmness and authority that I did not recognize my own voice. Several of my companions stopped. I repeated my appeal. We seized pickaxes which had been abandoned by the deported laborers and ran toward the storehouse.

Two S.S. guards on bicycles passed, but we paid no attention to them. We began to demolish the door. Soon we had what we wanted from the bread supply.

Now a fit of destructive rage seized us. We were intoxicated

196

with our success. We had actually destroyed something in a place where we had hitherto been the victims of other people's desire to destroy!

"Down with the camp!" we cried, half crazed. "Down with the camp! Long live liberty!"

That scene was the realization of so many of my dreams. How many times, tortured by hunger, had I said to my companions, "And when the Russians are near, we will pillage the bread stocks."

"Oh, that is your set ideal," they used to reply, laughing.

When we had sufficient provisions, I hurried to the barrack and settled my affairs. My parcel was ready; my blanket was rolled and knotted at both ends like a soldier's pack.

I was in a frenzy of emotion. My cheeks were on fire. The enemy was ready to collapse. I had assisted in the first movement toward the liberation of this oppressed, debased, decimated mass.

We fairly hopped toward the exit of the camp. From afar we could hear detonations. Were those cannons rumbling?

Thirty guards stood at the gates. Before letting us out, they examined us one by one under a pocket flashlight, in what became another selection. Those who were judged to be too old or too feeble were driven back into the camp.

Once we were outside the camp we had to line up, as always, in columns of five. A new period of waiting began. This lasted for about two hours, for the whole convoy was to consist of six thousand women.

Then the S.S. closed the gates. An order was barked. Our column was under way. Was it possible? We were leaving Birkenau still alive!

After we had traveled some distance, we came to a turn in the road. Here we looked back for our last glimpse of Birkenau where we had suffered such unbelievable trials.

I recalled that evening when, surrounded by my loved ones, I had arrived here. An ocean of light had bathed the camp.

197

Now everything was plunged into darkness; and only burning embers, where the crematory records were being incinerated, feebly lighted the barracks, the miradors, and the barbed-wire fences.

I thought of my parents, of my children, of my husband. Grief and remorse which had not left me for an instant tightened their fierce grips on my heart. Ah, my duty was clear. I must avenge them. For that I must regain my liberty. Now I would escape — if I could.

Not far off a mysterious rumbling started. We were told that an artillery duel was under way some distance beyond the forest. Then our liberators were *within shelling range!*

The S.S. hurried us along, and the lights grew dimmer and dimmer. Birkenau, the greatest slaughterhouse in human history, was little by little disappearing from view.

198

CHAPTER XXVI

Freedom

Surrounded by S.S. guards, we were herded along Auschwitz Road. It was freezing cold, and the air knifed through our rags. Shots rang out in the distance. The firing of big guns became louder; the detonations seemed to be closer and echoed with rapidity! Intermittent bursts of rockets lit up the skies. The Russians were evidently mounting a grand assault. We became gayer as the night was rent by the brilliant lights. The distant hammering of the artillery was the best farewell music to Auschwitz.

They drove us faster and faster. The German guards became alarmed. They whipped us into a run until we no longer felt the cold, our clothes were so drenched with perspiration. The dogs, as though sensing danger to their masters, were viciously tense. They bared their fangs and snarled at us, ready to attack anyone who fell out of the column.

The camp, which not long ago had been ablaze with incandescence, had sunk into the darkness. A few hours earlier we had looked forward to this march. Now, as we trudged on, we wondered where we were being taken. What new vicious deeds would the Germans perpetrate before we were saved? Despite our experience during the past months, we could not anticipate the horrors that awaited us.

We were six thousand women marching over that snow-covered country road. Every few feet we saw corpses with splattered skulls. Other groups of prisoners had evidently preceded us. We concluded that the S.S. guards had become more brutal than ever. We sought no reasons; we were accustomed to see killings without reason from these men who had deteriorated into beasts.

That first day I noticed that several of my fellow prisoners lagged behind at the edge of the road and asked to be allowed to ride in the horse-drawn cart which was driven by a German guard and accompanied our group. I told myself that they were right. I should do likewise and save my strength. Then I observed that from time to time the cart would fall back to the rear of the column. When it reappeared, the prisoners riding in it were not the same people. What had happened to the others? I shuddered.

The tragedy of a fellow doctor made me realize the dreadful truth in its full reality. This was the case of Dr. Rozsa, the Czech doctor, who was an elderly woman. Her vitality ebbed quickly. I tried to encourage and to assist her, but she could not keep up and drifted farther and farther back toward the rear of the column. Her strength began to fail completely. She begged me to leave her to her fate and go on. I insisted upon staying, but she would not permit it.

After much urging I finally left. I thought I was leaving her to an uncertain fate, but not to certain death. Suddenly I looked back and saw the five S.S. guards at the rear of the column. The center guard turned and stretched out his right arm toward Dr. Rozsa, who stood in the middle of the road. When she realized what the German gesture meant she lifted her hands to her eyes in horror. A sharp crack echoed. Dr. Rozsa lay dead in the road.

Now I understood what fate awaited those who lagged behind or were taken into the cart. Now I realized why there had been one hundred and nineteen corpses. I had counted them within a twenty-minute walk. I had not tallied the bodies that lay in the ditches on both sides.

The S.S. guards were armed with machine guns and hand

200

grenades. Their orders were, that in the event of a Russian surprise, the six thousand prisoners were to be killed at once so the Russians could not liberate any of them.

I saw that we were truly marching to death. Again speculations on escape began to brew in my mind. My brain became feverish. I decided I must not be the only one to escape. I hurried to my friends Magda and Lujza, and told them what I had seen and what I planned. They were ready to follow me, but we had to wait a favorable moment.

In the meantime, we passed several Polish villages. I can never express the feelings which the sight of normal civilian life created in me. Homes with curtained windows behind which free people lived. The name-plate of a doctor noting regular office visiting hours.

In the interim many of our fellow internees had dropped out. We tried to stay in the front ranks, so that, if we were to stop for a moment, we would not fall to the rear.

Our section of the marchers passed the first night in a stable. My friends and I awoke before the others, for we wished to be in the first rank of the column. It was still dark. We had hardly formed our row when the first five ranks ahead of us, led by the S.S., moved off separately. Cries to halt were shouted at them, but this dissident group continued on determinedly. As a result my friend and I found ourselves in the first rank of the main column. Several Polish prisoners who were near us became quarrelsome. Indeed, the entire atmosphere became unbearable and increased my determination to escape. Beckoning to my companions, I stepped from the ranks and ran after the dissidents' group. However, they were moving rapidly, and we could not overtake them.

Our plight now was acute. We had burned our bridges behind us. Where should we turn? We could not go back. Since it was dark, the guards had not noticed our leaving, but they had seen our vague running shapes, and were yelling! *"Stehen bleiben!"*

Throughout the entire trek, except for curses and *"Stehen bleiben!"* or *"Veiter gehen!"* we heard no words. These commands were generally taken up and repeated in thunderous choruses by the thousands of prisoners. I thought I'd grow mad hearing those words repeated over and over. But now the words were punctuated by the crack of bullets. There was no chorus any longer. I might die, but this time I must escape.

I was sorry for Magda and Lujza. They were frightened, but they continued to follow me. From time to time we threw ourselves to the ground or crouched behind snow mounds to escape the volleys which the German guards fired. Fortunately, the dawn had not yet lightened the sky. At last, creeping and crawling, we came to a bend in the road and found cover.

We sighted a church steeple. Toward it we made our way. When we reached the little Polish village, we ran toward the church.

A man was standing in a doorway. From our rags he recognized that we must have escaped, but he pointed to a house. The gesture implied that we would find refuge there.

In the meantime, a German security patrol approached the church yard. When we saw the soldiers, we rushed to the house. It was a fairly large structure. Near the main building stood a barn. The door was closed, but there was a narrow opening in one wall — as though Providence had created it this very moment. We managed to crawl in. We climbed to the loft, which was filled almost to the roof, and hid in the hay. The German patrols, who may have seen our running shadows, dashed into the yard. But fortunately they were looking for several boys. The mistress of the house told them that there were no strangers on the premises; perhaps the guards had seen three of her own sons. Nevertheless, the Germans searched the entire house. Then they approached the barn. But for some unaccountable reason they decided to call off the search, promising to return later in the evening.

We hardly had a moment to rejoice over our good fortune

when a servant girl climbed to the hay loft and discovered us. Her employer followed. He declared that he would not inform the Germans, but we would have to leave. A long conversation followed, and the landlord relented somewhat. He agreed to let us stay in the barn that day and night while he, in the meantime, would seek out another hiding place. His wife, who was a kindly woman, fetched us food. So long had it been since we had eaten civilized provisions that we could not identify it. After much reflection I realized that it was simply bread spread with lard or grease. Only bread with grease, in a barn — but among free people. It was manna in Paradise.

Early the next morning our host awakened us. We were to follow him to our new hiding place. However, he warned us that if we encountered a German patrol he would ignore us, and we were not to recognize him.

His words of caution proved useful. A German patrol did cross our path. That instant, however, a rocket, apparently from the approaching Russian army, burst in the air and pinned the German guards to the ground. That moment we fled to the house that was to be our next refuge.

Our new host let us hide in the stable. But the next day, he allowed us into the best room, which was a bedchamber.

Here the old couple, their daughter, and Magda crowded into the beds while Lujza and I slept on the floor. German soldiers were also billeted here, for the surrounding countryside was still under occupation. Obviously it was not wise to leave the room.

One morning when I thought the Germans were away, I went into the kitchen to bake a batch of Transylvania cookies for the family. I was thus engaged when a German soldier unexpectedly entered the kitchen. He gazed at me in surprise and began to question me. Who was I and why had he not seen me before? I told him that I was a relative who had just arrived for a visit. That my mother was ill and bedridden in one of the village houses, and that I was generally occupied in nursing her.

Whether or not the soldier believed me, from that moment on he forced his hated companionship on me and on the family. Occasionally he brought me chocolates. One time he arrived with several friends and compelled me to join them in their parlor games. My friends, watching from the other room, observed with sympathy while I had to socialize with men whom I loathed and despised as the murderers of my loved ones.

The cannonading became louder. The Russians were undoubtedly advancing. The Germans who were quartered here received orders and prepared to retreat. I saw how and where they planted their mines and even witnessed a premature explosion which killed two soldiers.

From my conversations with these men I perceived that they considered the situation gloomy. But they were unwilling to admit that the battle was lost. They repeated over and over that the Reich was far too strong to lose the "final ultimate victory." We were not surprised to hear that, for a combat newspaper was printed in the locality to bolster their morale.

During the first week we saw it, the combat weekly still recorded military advances. The following week it announced that Germany was in danger but that "German heroes would save her." A week later it claimed that, "Providence would save Germany because Germany always acted in the name of Providence."

Perhaps fate had intended that I, who had survived a concentration camp and the horrors of the evacuation, should see the retreat of the beaten Wehrmacht. I shall never forget the night when the last sappers, in their white hooded caps, deadly tired, arrived in this little Polish house. They sat in the best room, in the kitchen, everywhere; eating and drinking everything they saw or could lay their hands on. The snow dripped from their white caps. Perhaps they were never served so willingly since the birth of the Third Reich as they were that evening. They were sitting at their own wake, and I felt a joy I had never before known as I watched these tired supermen bowed over

204

their rifles or leaning against a wall, or even lying on the floor, fast asleep. Yet my joy was short-lived. For when they left in retreat, the Germans took a great number of women from the village, and I was among the captives. For three days I was bound to a cart by my hands, and, like a slave, I was compelled to go along.

Only the sights I saw along the march saved me from losing my mind. The roads were crowded with the fleeing Germans and their collaborators, who, after years of robbing and looting, could hardly take their spoils with them. The retreating soldiers fled in dismay and panic: trucks carrying guns and machine guns; frightened, riderless horses stampeded; whole villages of people were driven before the German horses; and the Red Cross trucks, so feared in Auschwitz, now carried German wounded to a safer area. Everything indicated chaos. Total capitulation could be but a matter of days.

A new thought entered my mind and nearly drove me frantic. The little Polish village which I had just left was probably liberated by now. I began to gnaw at the ropes which bound my hands.

Several of the young mothers and girls who were bound with me to the carts could not stand the cold, the hunger, and the terror of the forced march, and died on the way. These corpses were not untied, but simply dragged along. The Germans paid attention to nothing; their only thought was to escape this threatened region.

Our third night we again spent in a stable. The Germans threw themselves upon the ground. The majority were drinking. My captor secured a few bottles and also began to imbibe. It was late at night when the result of my three days of constant gnawing at the ropes was rewarded with success, and the ropes fell from my wrists. But my gums were sore and bleeding, and my front teeth felt broken.

Everyone was in a deep, tired sleep, and their snoring disguised every other sound. I tried to steal out of the sleeping crowd, but the driver of the cart to which I had been bound raised himself from the floor on his elbow. He was drunk, yet rational enough to shoot if he thought I was trying to escape. But it was either his life or mine. I seized one of the bottles lying nearby, and with all my strength I swung it against his skull. The glass splintered, and the German fell forward on his face. On the threshold of the stable I looked back, but he did not move. I was sick with disgust. Even the thought of killing a hated Nazi gave me a dreadful feeling.

The scene outside on the road had not changed, except that perhaps there were more German soldiers in desperate retreat. I dared not go in the opposite direction, for that would attract suspicion. I tried the back roads, but they, too, were jammed with men hurrying in the same direction. There was no alternative but to hide between the houses and try to elude the soldiers.

I had been hiding for what seemed hours when I finally spied a woman. I mustered courage and spoke to her. But German soldiers were still in her house, and she could not take me in. However, she led me to a river and pointed to a brightly lit house on the other side. If I could swim across I would be safe, she said. The Germans were now evacuating that little village.

It was February. The river was choked with large ice floes. Besides, day was breaking. Soon it would be too dangerous to be seen swimming the river. I thought of Auschwitz. There I had believed in always taking a chance. So I started down the bank. I had survived the gas chambers; I would survive the river.

As I descended the good peasant woman crossed herself and covered her eyes with her hands. Fully clothed as I stood, I plunged into the ice-cold water.

It was almost dawn when I reached the opposite bank. The village was not yet liberated, but the Germans were indeed leaving, and the brightly lit house was empty. Later I learned that the inhabitants were hiding in caves because their village, in the middle of a forest, was the center of a heavy attack, with both the Germans and the Russians shelling the area. A terrify-

206

ing battle ensued, but it reached its climax as night fell. The Russians dropped their "Stalin candles," and for a minute the place was bathed in lights.

Outside I was enjoying this unforgettable scene. I was too fascinated and, perhaps, too frightened to run. Under the bombardment, houses disappeared in a few moments. The flying bullets from both sides made a weird music. Yet I could distinguish the excited neighing of horses, the noise of rushing motor cars, and even shouting voices. From the right, where the Russians were, the voices became louder, and at the same time the noises on the left lessened. German power was indeed diminishing. The Wehrmacht was in retreat again.

The master of the house, who claimed to have seen me approach, came after me. He was certain that I had been killed in the shelling. When the peasants, pouring out from their caves with red cheeks and brimming eyes, saw me, they thought that I was related to the evil one and averted their faces. I made no attempt to explain what the sight of a victory over the Germans could mean to me.

The consensus of opinion in the village was that it would still be three days before the Russians would arrive. Yet that same night Russian shock troops broke through and took possession of it.

The face of the little village changed immediately. Not long ago we had seen the Wehrmacht and the S.S. and had heard German commands everywhere. Now we heard a new language, a language foreign to us, and saw people we had never seen before; but they had brought us the greatest gift that life can give — liberty!

CHAPTER XXVII

I Still Have Faith

Looking back, I, too, want to forget. I, too, yearn for sunshine and peace and happiness. But it is not easy to erase memories of Gehenna when the roots of life have been destroyed and one has nothing living to go back to. In setting down this personal record I have tried to carry out the mandate given to me by the many fellow internees at Auschwitz who perished so horribly. This is my memorial to them. God rest their poor souls! No hell anyone could conceive could equal what they endured.

Frankly, I want my work to mean more than that. I want the world to read and to resolve that this must never, never be permitted to happen again. That after perusing this account any will still doubt, I cannot believe. Even as I pen my last words, figures rise before me and mutely plead that I tell their stories, too. I can resist the men and the women, but there are the phantoms of the little children . . . . the little snow men . . . .

On December 31, 1944, the S.S. High Command asked the camp of Birkenau for a general report on the interned children. Despite the original selections, there were still too many of these children who had been torn from their families. The Germans decided that they must disappear — and that it must be done quickly and cheaply.

Should the children be thrown into a concrete pit with gasoline poured over them and a firebrand applied, as always before?

No, gasoline was scarce. And munitions were needed at the front.

But the Germans never lacked resourcefulness. We received the order to "bathe" the children. At Birkenau one did not discuss an order. One carried it out no matter how revolting it might be.

On the endless lagerstrasse, the road to calvary of so many millions of martyrs, the little prisoners started out in a long procession. Their hair was cropped short. They tramped barefoot, in rags. The snow had melted underfoot, and the camp road was coated with ice. Some of the youngsters fell. Each fall brought a slashing blow from a cruel whip.

Suddenly, it was snowing again. The children, their rags sprinkled with white flakes, staggered on toward death. They were silent under the blows, silent like so many little snowmen. On they went, shivering, unable to cry any more, resigned, exhausted, terrified.

Little Thomas Gaston fell. His large brown eyes, bright with fever, seemed fascinated by the horsewhip, and followed its snarling motion in the air above him. The blows fell, but little Thomas was burning with fever. He had no strength left either to cry or to obey. We picked him up and carried him in our arms. He had been beaten so many times.

A raucous cry tore at the silence. *"Stehen bleiben!"* (Stop!) We arrived at the showers.

In the next few minutes, with neither soap nor towels, we had to "bathe" the children in the icy water. We could not dry them. We put their rags back on their poor dripping bodies and sent them into the usual columns — to wait. That was the device which the ingenious Germans employed to "solve" the children's problem, the problem of the innocents of Birkenau.

When all the children were "bathed," the roll call was taken. That took five long hours that day, five hours after a so-called bath in ice-cold water, while the children stood at attention in the freezing cold and snow.

"Little Jesus will come for you presently!" sneered a German guard at one child who was waiting with blue lips, utterly benumbed.

Few of the children of Birkenau survived that roll call. Those who did were to fall later under the blows of the German cudgels. And they were mostly "Aryan," too; but Polish, and therefore not of the "master race."

At last we were ordered back. As we marched on the camp street, spades and pickaxes were stilled for a moment as our fellow prisoners, who were working on the road, looked on. The S.S. swung their whips. We dragged the children along faster.

"Mother!" stammered little Thomas Gaston. His little body, tormented by fever, was already in the throes of death . . . .

Finally we returned to the barracks. The surviving children were like automatons, almost dead from exhaustion. But in this state they were driven back to the cold stables. Little Thomas died on the way, as did hundreds of others. We who had carried him had to put his little corpse out behind the barrack, according to the regulations, though we knew big, horrible rats were waiting for his still-warm flesh.

It was New Year's Eve . . . . Huge snowflakes were falling . . . . We could hear the rats . . . . We could only shut our eyes, and pray for justice . . . . *justice!* New Year's Eve . . . . Somewhere on earth, beyond the barbed wires, free men were shaking hands and raising their glasses to wish each other a Happy New Year! At Birkenau rats were feeding on the children of Europe.

The reader may ask, "What can I personally do that such dread things may never be repeated?" I am neither a political scientist nor an economist. I am a woman who suffered, lost her husband, parents, children, and friends. I know that the world must share the guilt collectively. The Germans sinned grievously, but so did the rest of the nations, if only through refusing to believe and to toil day and night to save the wretched and the dispossessed by every possible means. I know that if

210

people everywhere resolve that henceforth justice must be indivisible, that no Hitlers must ever be allowed to rise again, it will help. Certainly everyone whose hands were directly, or indirectly, stained with our blood must pay for his or her crimes. Less than that would be an outrage against the millions of innocent dead.

I recall endless discussions of student days when we used to seek an answer to the question: Fundamentally, is man good or bad? At Birkenau one was tempted to reply that he was unalterably bad. But this was a confirmation of the Nazi philosophy; that humanity is stupid and evil and needs to be driven with the cudgel. Perhaps the greatest crime the "supermen" committed against us was their campaign, often successful, to turn us into monstrous beasts ourselves.

To achieve such a degradation, they employed a stupid, brutalizing and disconcertingly useless discipline, incredible humiliations, inhuman privations, the constant menace of death, and, finally, a sickening promiscuity. The entire policy was calculated to reduce us to the lowest moral level. And they could boast of results: men who had been lifetime friends ended up by hating each other with real repugnance; brothers fought each other for a crust of bread; men of formerly unimpeachable integrity stole whatever they could; and often it was the Jewish kapo who beat his fellow Jewish sufferer. At Birkenau, as in the society extolled by the Nazi philosophers, the theory that "might makes right," prevailed. Power alone carried respect. The feeble and the aged could not dare hope for pity.

Each camp, each barrack, each koia was a little jungle apart from the others, but all were subject to the man-eating standards. To reach the summit of the pyramid in each of these jungles, one had to become a creature after the image of the Nazis, devoid of all scruples, especially of all feelings of friendship, solidarity, and humanity.

In Egypt, the slaves who built the pyramids and died at their work might at least have seen their structure, the work of their hands, rising always a little higher. The prisoners of Auschwitz-Birkenau who carried piles of stone, only to drag them to their original places the next day, could see but one thing: the revolting sterility of their effort. The weaker individuals sank more and more into an animal existence where they dared not dream of eating their fill, but only of taking the worst edge off their gnawing hunger. All they asked was to be a little less cold, to be beaten a little less often, to have a bit of straw to cushion the rough boards of the koia, and occasionally to have a whole glass of water for themselves even though it came from the polluted water supply of the camp. One required an extraordinary moral force to teeter on the brink of the Nazi infamy and not plunge into the pit.

Yet I saw many internees cling to their human dignity to the very end. The Nazis succeeded in degrading them physically, but they could not debase them morally. Because of these few, I have not entirely lost my faith in mankind. If, even in the jungle of Birkenau, all were not necessarily inhuman to their fellowmen, then there is hope indeed.

It is that hope which keeps me alive.

Glossary

ARBEITDIENST — internee who assigned work for Kommandos

AUSSENKOMMANDO — inmates who worked outside the camp

BEKLEIDUNGSKAMMER — the inmates' clothing warehouse

BLOCOVA — the barrack or block chief

CALIFACTORKA — the blocova's personal maid

"CANADA" — warehouse where articles taken from deportees were stored for shipment to Germany

KAPO — kommando chief

FUEHRERSTUBE — S.S. offices

ESSKOMMANDO — the food carriers

HAEFTLING — inmate of camp, or internee

KOMMANDO — work group

LAGERKAPO — lageraelteste's assistant

LAGERAELTESTE — Uncrowned "queen of the camp"

LAGERSTRASSE — chief road inside the camp

LAGERRUHE — curfew

MUSULMAN — the walking skeletons

OBERARZT — chief S.S. physician of the camp

"ORGANIZATION" — stealing from the Germans

RAPPORTSCHREIBERIN — chief secretary of the camp

POLITISCHE BUERO — political bureau where documents and records were kept

SCHREIBSTUBE — offices whence roll call reports went

SCHEISSKOMMANDO — latrine-cleaning group

SCHREIBERIN — scribe

STUBENDIENST — barrack gendarmerie; also food dividers

"SPORT" — punishment for blocovas, officials, and kitchen girls

SONDERKOMMANDO — special work group, here used to mean crematory workers

SONDERBEHANDLUNG (S.B.) — special handling, meaning "condemned to death"

SCUTZHAEFTLING — "protected" prisoners

VERTRETERIN — blocova's lieutenant

CPSIA information can be obtained
at www.ICGtesting.com
Printed in the USA
BVHW031345210520
580097BV00002B/113

9 781684 223930